"Finally, a reader-friendly and practical guide to helping people und⟨ attachment theory. This book provides the reader with hope and a cle⟨_ in their relationship with addiction. If you are someone or know someone struggling to find a way out of addiction, I highly recommend this book."

  —**Joel S. Porter, PsyD**, senior clinical lecturer at the National Addiction Centre at
    the University of Otago, NZ, and adjunct associate professor at the Centre for
    Applied Psychology at the University of Canberra, AU

"This book is a critical addition to the recovery literature. It offers challenging, yet nonjudgmental and insightful tools to propel recovering people on their journey to looking deeper at the root causes of their addiction, and steers them toward a deeper connection in their relationships so that they can finally heal."

  —**Stefanie Carnes, LMFT, CST, CSAT-S**, author of *Facing Addiction*

"Michael Barnett embraces his readers, taking them by the hand and guiding them gently through this detailed but easy-to-follow book. He reassures them that their addictions are not a weakness, but are rather their best—sometimes even lifesaving—coping strategy. He offers them the hope that the work of developing secure relationships is what can finally inoculate them against the turbulence of the addictive process in their lives."

  —**Avrum Weiss, PhD**, award-winning author of *Hidden in Plain Sight*

"Michael Barnett has thoughtfully and comprehensively applied the tenets of emotionally focused therapy (EFT) to the persistently vexing question of how best to treat substance use disorders and other addictions. While we have made great strides over the past twenty years in understanding the neurobiology of addiction, we have needed an approach that addresses addictions as symptoms of underlying emotional and trauma-related conditions. Michael has done that beautifully in this workbook."

  —**James A. Peck, PsyD**, licensed clinical psychologist, and senior clinical trainer in the
    division of addiction psychiatry at the David Geffen School of Medicine at UCLA

"Michael Barnett charts a clear path out of the pernicious and perplexing challenges of addiction, offering readers a compassionate journey through the despair of painful isolation to the hope found in a loving connection with self and others. Through his insights and experience, this gifted therapist and soulful guide offers profound wisdom, practical advice, and proven practices that lift the spirit, connect the heart, and give breath to life."

  —**James Furrow, PhD**, couple and family therapy program at Seattle University,
    and director of the EFT Center of Seattle

The
Emotionally
Focused Therapy
Workbook for Addiction

How to Heal the Loneliness and Shame
That Trigger Addictive Behaviors

MICHAEL BARNETT, LPCC

New Harbinger Publications, Inc.

NEW HARBINGER PUBLICATIONS is a registered trademark of New Harbinger Publications, Inc.

New Harbinger Publications is an employee-owned company.

Copyright © 2024 by Michael Barnett
New Harbinger Publications, Inc.
5720 Shattuck Avenue
Oakland, CA 94609
www.newharbinger.com

Cover design by Amy Daniel

Acquired by Wendy Millstine

Developed by Jess O'Brien

Edited by Marisa Solis

Printed in the United States of America

26   25   24

10   9   8   7   6   5   4   3   2   1   First Printing

Contents

Foreword

It is with a special pleasure to witness Michael Barnett's labor of love through these last many years, culminating in this book that heartfully consolidates an attachment approach to working with addiction through the lens of the concepts, practices, and processes of emotionally focused therapy (EFT).

I fondly recall many conversations between the two of us when Michael first began researching the implementation of EFT within the treatment protocol of a reputable treatment facility in Atlanta, Georgia, many years ago. What began as a rough sketch for providing a path forward for people struggling with addiction has evolved into a clear, well-thought-out approach to healing addiction from the inside out.

For more than a century, the puzzle of how to support people suffering from addiction has been much like a Zen koan to the fields of both psychotherapy and mental health. Although we have marveled at medical breakthroughs that allow us to understand the neurobiology of addiction in exquisite detail, hundreds of thousands of people continue to suffer and even die each year from addictive-related causes. The vast majority of contemporary approaches available to us address the problem of addiction from the top down, assessing it solely as a behavior to be modified. Michael illuminates what has been missing from the field that has essentially been right under our noses the entire time: human connection as the primary resource for healing.

Human connection—attachment—offers the clearest, most direct, and potent promise for not only supporting the healing of the pain that causes addiction but a resource to heal the suffering of the human being. Through EFT, Michael provides readers with effective tools to navigate the turbulent emotional aspects of themselves responsible for self-medication into a new world of possibility: a sense of belonging, connection, and relief without substances.

In doing so, Michael has elevated approaching addictive processes beyond the traditional framework of fellowship, which is necessary but far from sufficient. Like a potent tide pulling the waters to the shoreline, Michael's inviting voice pulls people beyond simply stopping addictive behavior toward the hidden realities of their own emotional worlds. The inner terrain of emotion can be treacherous and overwhelming for even the most resourced and balanced of people; sadly, when addiction has made its presence palpable in people's lives, finding the doorway in, where healing must occur, is all but impossible.

Michael has a knack for walking people gently, yet persistently, into the experience of their emotional selves so that they can unlock the doorways that have prevented them from healing their pasts through love and relationship rather than through their substances of choice. Michael's extraordinarily effective step-by-step process guides each reader into a lovely process of discovery of the emotional truths that have been driving their addictive processes.

It is with great pleasure to have the opportunity to celebrate Michael's contribution to the field of addiction through offering such a caring, sensitive, and human approach to helping people find their own way to transform their relationship with addiction.

—Susan Johnson, EdD
Founder and creator of emotionally focused therapy

Prologue

Writing this book holds deep meaning for me. It is a gift, my gift to you and hopefully to many others who know the suffering, pain, and isolation not just simply from addiction but from the pain *beneath* the addictive processes that no one sees: the private hurt that all of us who have struggled with addiction are intimately acquainted with that goes unnoticed by the world at large. In the outside world, people tend to see what is on the surface. They make judgmental assumptions and interpretations about our personal character and intentions based upon what they think they see and know. Unbeknownst to them, there is an unseen, vulnerable, and deeply human world beneath the surface that may be well hidden from view where every misinformed perception rubs more salt deeply into the well-disguised wounds that lurk beneath our "social" exteriors. What is missed, and gravely overlooked, is the hurting human that lies buried within.

I remember my first time getting high. It was *amazing*! I felt relaxed, playful, giddy, and...cool. I was vibing with my friend, laughing and talking a lot, and experiencing a whole new wonderful world of awe, wonder, and connection. It felt as if we had entered a brand-new, delightful, mysterious world together. We had somehow unlocked an invisible door that gave way to a joy that was completely devoid of the all-encompassing angst and confusion that was my familiar companion. This magical world was not only hidden from adults and authorities, but something so foreign to them that we could call it our own without any confining instructions or pressure to deflate the joy that we had found. It was all ours, and it was quite incredible!

On one hand, this sounds wonderful, even blissful. Wouldn't everyone wish for experiences like this? However, as these words emerge on the page, a deep sadness washes over me: I was thirteen years old at the time...

Like many of us during childhood, I was frequently met with judgments and criticisms from those around me. "What is wrong with you?" was the most common question thrown my way. The harsh consequences and derogatory comments from the people entrusted with my care and guidance cut deeply into my sense of self. However, the added burden of shame to my already heavy heart was the worst "punishment" of all.

Very little meaningful and effective professional help was available then, and sadly the same holds true today. The vast majority of books and resources available to people seeking to heal from addictive processes offer skills and cognitive practices that serve as guardrails to pull in the reins of addiction. Although some of these practices may place a stopgap to using, they tend to fall apart during crucial moments of needing to keep our recovery strong and solid—they rarely touch the murky reservoir of pain within the heavy hearts of those of us struggling with addiction. This leaves us caught in the endless merry-go-round of relapse and addiction.

Despite many attempts to get clean, internal "pep talks," and all the tools and resources available, I couldn't access—let alone heal—the distress that churned inside of me. Although I could stop using for periods of time, the skills and tools at my disposal weren't able to dissipate the heaviness within me. Sadly, I returned to substances again and again to quiet the turmoil, which continued to erode my sense of self-worth and adequacy.

Your circumstances may be different. Perhaps you were quite aware why you were in so much pain and despair. Perhaps you knew in your bones that there was no one who could soften that jagged hurt that resides deep down inside. Either way, the awful combination of not just hurting, *but hurting alone*, made both your pain and your problems exponentially more overwhelming. With all this pain, the relief that addictive substances and behaviors provide makes a hell of a lot of sense. The reason addiction is everywhere boils down to one consistent truth about addiction: it works.

Until it doesn't... Addiction takes on a life of its own and viciously pulls us into its downward spiral. This is most likely why we are meeting here within the pages of this book.

So, fast forward: I am now happily married, successful as a father, and have wonderful friends and community, as well as meaningful work. I have been working in the field of psychology for more than three decades. I, like many of my peers, entered the field to answer some very deep and personal questions: *What is wrong with me? Why do I feel this way? Is there a way out? Can I find relief? Can I be happy and feel alive? And can I ultimately help others to do the same?*

These are the questions that can only be answered through embarking on our own personal journey to heal our emotional self. The inward journey grants us access to those places within us that hold the hurt that drives addiction in the first place. This book is intended to work well with any of the skill sets that you have previously learned and take you further into your healing process, so that you won't need addiction the way you have in the past.

The field of psychology and personal growth unexpectedly provided a rich and rewarding path for my journey, one that I am grateful to have embraced wholeheartedly. It took time. It required risk. It wasn't easy at first. However, if I hadn't taken the risk, I believe that I would still be lost. The journey that helped me to identify, encounter, and eventually embrace the emotional world within myself allowed me to finally lean into—and later come into genuine harmony with—the things that I most feared.

I couldn't have done this alone. There is no way to do so. The greatest gift of growth and healing has been the sacred people along the way who have helped me to not feel alone. They gave me the courage to move forward. They inspired me. They loved me when I could not love myself.

Whether personally or professionally speaking, I am the fruits of my soul journey. I join you here not as a remote ivory tower expert, but instead as a wounded healer who learned that *there is real hope and transformation possible for all of us.*

My hurt, pain, and confusion became my greatest teachers. I propose that yours can be the same for you. My journey has had many twists and turns, trials and tribulations, as well as beautiful moments of grace, good fortune, and luck. I've come face to face with tragedies, losses, failures, and freak-outs. At times, life left me drowning in a quagmire of despair. However, I knew there had to be something different, something better out there. With the help of caring others, I was able to face my pain, find ways of making sense of it...and ultimately experience the genuine transformation of pain into wisdom. Wisdom is the ineffable experience of turning lead into gold, lemons into lemonade, and deep pain into strength and understanding that remains intact for the rest of our lives. Wisdom is knowing truth in your very bones. It remains with us for the rest of our days.

I have had the great good fortune of being led to the invaluable and paradoxical discovery that opening Pandora's box, which for decades I kept deeply hidden away inside of myself like Fort Knox, became the royal road to the experience of well-being that I gratefully call "home" now. One of my heroes—the renowned author, scholar, and sage Joseph Campbell—implied in his writings that this journey is not for the faint of heart. He entitled the process "the hero's journey." I love that. But I believe that we are all heroes in disguise who haven't been given the tools, guidance, and wisdom for this transformational alchemy...yet.

Introduction

We are all too aware of the widespread prevalence of substance abuse and addiction, right? But how common is it, really?

In 2020, *40.3 million people aged 12 or older* in the United States (14.5 percent of the population) reportedly had a substance use disorder (SUD) in the past year (Lange et al. 2024). Despite more than one hundred years of scientific research, addiction has become to the field of behavioral health what the common cold is to the field of medicine: ubiquitous. It can affect anyone and occur at any time. Even with profound medical advances capable of mapping the impact of addiction on the brain in exquisite detail, addiction has escalated exponentially. In this very moment, as you open the pages of this workbook, you are among thousands of people earnestly seeking relief from addiction who have been unable to find a way out.

When we sincerely attempt to change our relationship to addiction and are unsuccessful, we diminish our self-esteem and further fuel the fires of addiction. Instead of being proud of making earnest efforts to change course, our failed attempts at quitting leave us with the brutal sting of disappointment. We let down the people we love (again), and we let down ourselves (again). Bearing the heavy burden of disappointing ourselves is deeply discouraging. Therefore, I want to extend a *huge congratulations to you for standing tall and picking up this book so that you can create real change in your own life.*

The pandemic laid bare the predictable correlation between isolation, dislocation (read "disconnection"), and *addiction.* While I was writing the proposal for this book, *The New York Times* published a heartbreaking headline that was a testament to this fact: "Overdose Deaths Reached Record High as Pandemic Spread." It went on to say, "the previously unimaginable benchmark of over 100,000 deaths caused by drug overdose was recorded in the United States over the past 12 months" (Rabin 2021). This is astounding. The previous benchmark for death by drug overdose was 70,630 people in the United States (National Center for Health Statistics 2021).

The reality is that we can never effectively treat addiction if we can't identify and understand its root cause. We know all too well that addiction is a powerful (and reliable) way to avoid and numb emotion. However, truth be told, *none of us* learned to avoid feeling our feelings randomly—we needed to keep them at bay for very good reasons, which we will get to later. Plain and simple, emotional pain without dependable people to offer reassurance and support means one must find another source of relief. For so many of us, drugs and alcohol become that option. Substances can offer temporary relief (at best) from emotional pain. However, in time, as you know all too well, addiction eventually takes on a life of its own. And it can be *deadly.* Alternatively, when life's road gets rocky, when we know in our bones that there are people to whom we can turn who care about us, we are infinitely stronger, more resilient, and safe.

This workbook is written to help you find a path into and through the very heart of the distress that set addiction in motion to begin with. It is a unique approach to healing the very source of what addictive processes have been attempting to self-medicate. This book is intended to offer you the help and guidance from ground zero, at addiction's emotional epicenter, so that you can heal it from the bottom up.

This workbook will not re-present the familiar tools that you have likely already attempted to utilize to change your relationship with addiction. It will provide you with a new understanding of your addiction, as well as powerful skills and processes for you to be able to recover your connection to yourself and others. Once you can see the path clearly, you can find the way through to the other side. Without a clear path, you end up lost in the woods without a compass. As baseball player Yogi Berra once said, "If you don't know where you are going, you will end up somewhere else."

Emotionally Focused Therapy (EFT): Transforming Addiction Through Attachment

So, what is the path? A profound and exciting resource for successfully transforming the underlying disease that silently propels addiction has been hiding in plain sight for all too long: the power of dependable human connection; the power of *attachment*.

This may sound more like a promotion for a valentine's day card than an effective approach for transforming addiction, but decades' worth of hard science, empirically validated research, and thousands of hours of both clinical and personal experience beg to differ. A brilliant psychotherapist named Dr. Susan Johnson created a model of therapy called emotionally focused therapy (EFT) and it is the most successful relational therapy ever researched (Johnson 2019; Spengler et al. 2022)! EFT harnesses the power of relationships so that you can thrive *without being held hostage to addiction*. It offers understandable concepts, approachable processes, and coping skills that can guide you on your path through addiction toward a state of health and well-being that is your birthright.

EFT's body of empirically validated research shows dramatic reductions in PTSD, depression, and anxiety (Weissman et al. 2018; Wittenborn et al. 2018). These are the *exact same underlying symptoms* consistently associated with addiction. They are the source of the pain—the ground zero—that primes ongoing addictive use.

So, here is our formula: *Let's heal the pain and trauma that lurk beneath the surface...and then we can heal the addiction that lives above it.* Without getting to the heart and origin of the emotional pain we have been trying to keep at bay, we remain vulnerable to relapse and the overwhelming power of addiction.

Grounded in the attachment-based tools of emotionally focused therapy, this workbook targets the hidden pain of loneliness, despair, and shame that can drive addiction, showing you how to build healthy attachment, belonging, connection, and safety with the ones you love as a buffer against drugs and alcohol.

In these pages you will find practical information about addictive processes and healing through the tenets, wisdom, and practical approaches found within EFT. EFT views addictive processes as an understandable and even functional (yes, you heard me!) strategy designed to manage and soothe our hidden emotional distress. None of us turns to drugs or alcohol randomly. Life doesn't always deal us the best hand of cards to play.

However, being adaptive creatures, we found the best way to play the hand we were dealt...now we're here to learn a new way.

This workbook will provide you with more than just hope. It will provide you with a compassionate, humanizing framework for understanding and normalizing your addiction. The exercises focus on developing effective ways of understanding and coping with your inner world of emotion, to create *emotional fluency*: the ability to identify what you feel and why you are feeling that way, and clearly express these feelings to others. Becoming emotionally fluent will offer you the ability to feel seen, heard, and understood by the people in your life. It is the language of *you*.

You will find a path forward as well as hands-on practices for how to use *attachment processes* to your advantage, so that you will be able to move through the dark places that have held you captive to addiction. Attachment processes refer to the bioevolutionary process of internalizing emotional awareness, resilience, and a strong sense of self through our ongoing development in relationship to healthy caregiving others. Our attachment relationships provide both a pathway and the "substance" that enriches our confidence, self-worth, and ability to be resilient in the face of life's twists and turns.

The skills, processes, and exercises in this workbook are based upon what is known as *felt security*. Felt security is that internal knowing in our bones that we are loved, supported, and at our core very good people. All of us struggling with addiction do not have that as our baseline foundation. This workbook will help you transform at that basic level. You'll build a firm foundation that will serve as your very own healthy buffer to the stress and impact of a changing, unpredictable, and, at times, very confusing world—without needing to use substances.

How to Use This Book

Sincere commitment to personal growth is based upon the adage: *you need to feel it in order to heal it.* Although the concept is simple, the process is not always easy. Humanizing addiction through the attachment lens will strengthen your ability to navigate the road of self-discovery even when the journey becomes a bit bumpy...and sometimes it does.

As you do the exercises, turning up the volume of your emotional world may be challenging at times. So, take it slow. Take it at your own pace. Most of the journey through this book will be enlightening, easily applicable, and empowering. You may also hit a few bumps when the process opens inner doors that you aren't as familiar with. When that happens it can stir up feelings that have been quietly residing within you.

Here are a few thoughts to support you having the most enjoyable and productive experience while reading this book:

- **Be curious and open.** Remember, this is a journey! This workbook offers skills, ideas, and exercises to help you grow and heal without using addictive processes. Approach each chapter and exercise with a spirit of curiosity and openness. You may get a bit stirred up as you take this journey into yourself. Please note: *That is A-OK*. Nothing is going wrong. Be open to where this experience takes you.

- **Do all the exercises.** Repeat them often (some daily) so you'll become familiar with them, strengthen your coping skills, and eventually develop an ongoing practice. You can find PDF versions of many of the worksheets online at http://www.newharbinger.com/52403. Print extra copies of the worksheets you want to do multiple times.

- **Offer yourself compassion.** Remember: this is a *no-judgment zone*. Be kind and generous with yourself as you contemplate and self-reflect. We are all playing the best game in town, doing the best with where we are at any given moment.

- **Pace yourself.** You will enjoy this book more, as well as get much more out of it, when you pace yourself accordingly. Only you can determine the most helpful rhythm of reading and engaging with the exercises for you. Pacing your process on the journey throughout this book is an invaluable part of that.

- **Take the risk of treading on new terrain.** Whenever we engage in emotional or personal-growth work we open the door to new and often hidden parts of ourselves and our own experience. Stirring up the proverbial dust in the corners can be both thrilling as well as a bit nerve-racking at times. You might feel a bit shaky or tense. This just means that you have courageously entered new emotional terrain. *New territory always becomes familiar ground once we spend enough time there.* This will happen for you too, and once it does you will have incorporated a new empowering resource into yourself! This is how we grow and heal.

- **Journal.** Take time to write about your experience. Writing both helps you internalize the work and unfolds your experience into a deeper sense of meaning and wisdom. Journaling is one of the most useful tools for processing and consolidating learning. Because so much of this book is designed to help you access new or hidden parts of yourself, journaling your experience helps the new become familiar, as it becomes a more solidified part of yourself through writing. You can think of your journaling practice as an intimate conversation with your inner self about the new horizons you are discovering and all the ways that you are growing and changing, without needing your addiction of choice.

Many exercises call for you to apply new skills and concepts to day-to-day activities. Pay attention to these encounters and take time several times a week to record and reflect upon them in your journal. (Yes, that last bullet point is so important that we'll spend a few more paragraphs on it.) In addition, twice a week take some time to free-write. That is, sit quietly and begin to write about what you are experiencing inside, what you are feeling. Turn your awareness inward to thoughts and feelings about how you are growing, where you are now, and where you would like to see yourself in the next two weeks, month, year... Forecast your growth as well as any obstacles you may be concerned about that could get in the way of successfully coming to terms with addiction.

If you do encounter a shaky-ground moment, take time to sit quietly and write about it too. What was losing your emotional balance really about? How do you understand this vulnerability from what you know about the scope of your life? How does the past possibly blur the present?

Finally, *always* conclude your journaling with uplifting, affirming comments for and about yourself. It really helps!

The Journey Ahead

This book is designed to be a journey for you and about you. Take great pride in the courage, strength, and humility that you are bringing to the experience of changing your relationship to addiction once and for all. It is extremely commendable. Congratulate yourself. I congratulate you! I look forward to walking alongside you throughout these pages.

CHAPTER 1

Addiction Redefined

We begin this book by getting clear on what addiction *is* and what it is *not*. Why? Because definitions influence the professional advice, guidelines, resources, and protocols for treatment that you may have already attempted to use. And if you are reading this book, my guess is that those resources have not helped you get where you want to go. There is a good reason for that. And we're about to change that for the better.

The purpose of this chapter is to help you more clearly understand why your previous attempts at changing your relationship with addiction may have been unsuccessful. It is intended to place you on a solid path forward that will help you achieve your goal of getting out of the clutches of addiction.

The Common Misconception About Addiction

The addiction treatment field—as well as the experts, counselors, and leaders within it—has not come to a conclusive perspective about the causes of addiction nor how to effectively treat it (Alexander 2008). Most of the leading opinions regarding the causes of addiction include a degree of stigma and judgment about a person's character or capability. An inherently shaming thread runs through most of our contemporary perspectives about addiction, leaving us feeling bad about ourselves. The shocking paradox is that the very protocols and processes that were designed to help break the chains of addiction have often been a source of shame and additional distress, which ironically further activates the need to self-medicate with substances (Finberg 2015).

For the record, we don't have character defects. We are not broken, diseased, lowly, or too weak to contend with chemicals and urges. We are human beings who have not always been dealt the easiest hand of cards. Therefore, we need a more complete and humane definition of addiction if we are to grow and heal in such a way that we can release the hold of addiction once and for all.

As we embark upon the journey in this workbook, let's begin by dispelling any stigma about addiction with a new, simple, and relatable definition of addiction.

A Revised Understanding of Addiction

When we cast stigmas and misconceptions aside, we can look more compassionately at addiction and ourselves. Here is a description I've found eliminates shame and gets to the truth: *Addictive processes help us cope with often-unbearable emotional suffering and distress when the support and care of dependable others is simply not an option.*

This revised understanding of addiction is both human and non-pathologizing. It acknowledges that life is challenging, that no one gets out unscathed. It views addiction for what it is: functional. Addiction serves a meaningful purpose: it helps us cope with emotional and personal suffering that, for some of us, is unbearable (Maté 2007). Ironically, addiction may have saved our lives. Addiction essentially stood in as a surrogate for the care and presence of loving, dependable others in our lives when such people and circumstances were simply not an option. Addiction may have prevented us from psychologically falling apart...or worse.

This new perspective offers hope and possibility. It provides a guide for creating healthy alternatives to lighten our load and helps prop us up when the going gets tough. In the chapters ahead we will talk about cultivating *secure attachment* in our lives, hearts, and relationships.

The bumps, bruises, and hardships of life are bearable only if we have the safe haven of community and caring others to lean into when the going gets tough. Although a sense of belonging within a community should be a birthright, it is far from a given. Therefore, I want you to know that your addiction is not your fault. However, changing your relationship with the addictive processes that have compromised your life *is your responsibility.*

The good news is that successfully accomplishing this is truly within your reach. You already have more internal resources and strengths than you give yourself credit for. The pages of this workbook will help you uncover and access them to use for your own recovery.

The Hidden Gifts of Addiction

Here is a legitimate question for you: What have you gotten out of using? Not what it has done for you, or what negative consequences have come with using, but rather, what has it given you that was previously absent from your life and your world? What has addiction provided for you? (Maté 2007). This is extremely important for you to consider and reflect upon.

For instance, using may have dulled the pain, loneliness, and dashed hopes that you have carried inside of you. Perhaps it has calmed you down or mellowed out the undercurrent of worries and pressures in your life. Maybe it has helped you to feel more connected with others rather than live in fear and isolation. These are just a few of the many possibilities of how addiction may have "gifted" you. Can you think of others?

Letter of Gratitude

Write a letter of gratitude to your addiction. This may sound like an insane request given that addiction has cost you so much in your life. However, through sincerely acknowledging and honoring the "gifts" that addiction offered, you are setting yourself squarely on the path to a world of successful recovery. Sincerely give thought to all the ways addiction helped you out. Write down at least six "gifts" that your addiction provided for you:

1. _____

2. _____

3. _____

4. _____

5. _____

6. _____

What was it like to list these gifts?

_____

_____

_____

_____

_____

_____

Now, incorporate the gifts that you identified into a letter of gratitude to addiction for the place that it held in your life.

Dear Addiction,

_____

_____

_____

_____

_____

_____

_____

_____

_____

_____

_____

_____

_____

_____

_____

_____

_____

How are you doing after writing your letter and sitting with your takeaways from a more compassionate perspective? I hope that you can begin to acknowledge more of your humanness as you recognize the core need that addiction was attempting to help you fulfill. The gifts that addiction was *trying* to provide are basically the gifts of being and *feeling* human.

Let's take this work a step further. You have discovered what your addiction was attempting to offer you. By definition, all those qualities and experiences must be absent in your day-to-day experience, or you wouldn't be consistently seeking them through using.

You have just revealed some of the missing and painful deficits in your life. Addiction is an attempt to gain what is missing. Identifying what those things are begins your journey of creating those experiences and qualities for yourself without needing to use to achieve them.

Identifying What Addiction Attempted to Fill

Return to the list of gifts you jotted down in the previous exercise and review what you wrote. Then, try to identify all the deficits, voids, and missing parts of your life that those gifts were responding to. What gaps in your life has your addiction been filling?

1. _____

_____

_____

2. _____

_____

_____

3. _____

_____

_____

4. _____

_____

_____

5. _____

_____

_____

6. _____

_____

_____

You have just identified the purpose and function of your using. You have just begun to acknowledge part of your story. It is a human story. Write down what it is like for you to acknowledge the beginning of this story of what your addiction has been attempting to solve.

_____

_____

_____

_____

_____

_____

Identifying the struggles and hardships that you have been living with, including using addiction to self-medicate, offers a starting point for healing those parts of you through other means. As you continue the journey through this book, you will encounter extraordinary options for healthy ways of metabolizing and letting go of the hurt and pain that you have been carrying all this time.

One of the best metabolizers of hurt and pain is a regular visualization practice. Visualizing healing experiences can be immensely powerful. Effective visualization literally impacts our psyche in growth-producing ways. You will be engaging in specific creative visualizations at different times throughout the journey of this book. But for now, let's create a simple practice to get you started.

Please note that this is a practice that you may find very simple and immediately effective, or if you're like me, it may take some time to be able to visualize clear images for yourself. With consistent practice, noticeable improvement occurs in a relatively short period of time. So, _be patient with yourself._ If you are unable to do this at first, remember, _nothing is going wrong._ It is simply part of the learning process. This practice will become both easier and stronger over time as long as you are consistent with it.

Beginning to Cultivate an Effective Visualization Practice

Practice this visualization exercise three times this week. Each time you engage, be patient with yourself. Allow five to ten minutes to relax into the experience. Bring as many of your senses into the experience as possible.

1. Find a quiet place where you can comfortably relax.

2. Breathing through your nose, take three deep breaths, breathing in nice and deep, and then exhaling fully. Rest in the third exhalation, allowing the breath to return to normal.

3. Begin your visualization by picturing planting the seed of a rose. Vividly picture the color of the soil, notice the feeling of your fingers placing the seed deeply inside the soil, notice how the soil becomes moist as you add some water to it. Take a moment to admire the rose that you have just planted.

4. Begin to visualize the seed taking in both water and sunlight, feeling the soil warming with the rays of the sun, and noticing the very beginning of life occurring as the first roots penetrate the seed's shell as they seek nourishment from the rich soil that you have placed it in.

5. Visualize roots spreading through the soil, creating a lovely anchor and channel for nutrients to feed your lovely rose. Also notice the green shoots struggling as they strive for daylight above the soil.

6. Picture the shoots breaking the surface of the soil. Notice the tender green color. Watch in your mind's eye the shoots growing and multiplying as they pierce the soil and take on the shape of the first stems of your rose.

7. Notice the stems branching out and buds beginning to show up.

8. Focusing on the bud taking in the warmth of the golden sun, notice how the bud begins to slowly form. Notice how it begins to gently open. Notice the color of the red rose bursting forth, notice the various folds and lines of the very beginnings of a petal before your eyes.

9. Notice the bud blossoming and opening as you distinctly see each and every leaf opening toward the rays of the sun. Notice the stamen and the follicles within it. And even notice the beautiful fragrance that it gives off.

10. See the rose, feel the soil, smell its fragrance, take in the warmth of the sun on your skin. Enjoy!

11. When you are ready, open your eyes and return to the present.

By starting a visualization practice—and committing to the exercises in this book—you have started down the path toward eliminating the need to self-medicate with addiction. Congratulations!

CHAPTER 2

Natural Recovery

Andrea worked as an entry-level counselor at a prestigious inpatient addiction treatment center. She and her coworkers became close and opened up about how their journeys led them to work in this field. Andrea quickly learned that she was a "unicorn," that she stood apart from the norm because, although she had stopped using, she had never gone to treatment or entered a 12-step program. She literally just stopped!

Andrea told me, "What surprised me was the consistency of my coworkers' responses to my history of using. They told me, 'For us, we would have died had we not gone into treatment,' 'If it weren't for the program, I'm not sure I would still be here today,' 'We can't believe that you never went to treatment!'"

Then Andrea talked about her own history. "I had a moment of reckoning as I was going out to cop one night," she said. "A very dark thought grabbed me: *If I keep going down the current path I am traveling, my life is going to go straight to hell.* So, I pulled over on the side of the road, and with my head resting against the cold steering wheel I sat in solemn self-reflection. The next thing I knew I was turning my car around and driving home empty-handed with tears that were a combination of grief and relief rolling down my cheeks. That was the end. I was done."

Andrea's story sounds incredibly unique, don't you think? She stopped just like that all on her own! I have heard many stories from friends and coworkers who all required treatment and the 12-step program to change their lives and embrace recovery. I assumed this was the norm, and that Andrea must be some kind of anomaly. Again and again, it seemed that people only stopped using through formal intervention. For decades, I believed that Andrea's story was an outlier...until I stumbled on a body of research called *natural recovery*.

Change Is Not Only Possible, It's Probable!

It may feel disorienting to discover that there is a vast body of epidemiological research (Hasin et al. 2007) revealing that the majority of people who struggle with addictive processes stop using on their own accord, without any form of professional intervention whatsoever. But it's true!

Natural recovery is an organic life process that leads to recovery without formal treatment or self-help groups. It typically involves struggling with strong feelings that one's using is incongruent with the kind of person they want to be, that is, discordant with their own values, aspirations, and life goals (Heyman 2009). Usually, natural recovery happens over a period of several years of attempting to stop but not yet achieving recovery goals...until one day the transformation of one's relationship to addiction is successful.

As it turns out, Andrea's story is shared by *most people* who have successfully changed their relationship to addiction. Learning this revolutionized the way that I view addiction. This new framework offers so much hope for those of us who have wrestled with addiction. Most of us have agonized for years over whether we would ever have the strength to successfully change the course of our lives. Feelings of failure are front and center each time we attempt to quit and find ourselves using again. We get trapped in that familiar vicious cycle of addiction that goes something like this: muster the courage and strength to stop using, make excuses, start using again, feel worse for not following through, and then use our drug of choice to cope with the pain of failing once again. Wash, rinse, repeat. Each repetition only strengthens the cycle's power over us.

Not knowing that most people recover naturally from addictive processes can leave you feeling doomed to having a very low ceiling on your life and personal aspirations. Research shows that 75 percent of people struggling with addiction successfully change their relationship to using substances and behaviors either through abstinence or harm reduction (Blanco et al. 2011; Peele and Zach 2019). When viewed through this lens, changing your relationship to your addiction becomes a genuine possibility—maybe more so than you have ever considered.

It is absolutely essential that you understand that you too are destined for recovery. There really is light at the end of the tunnel! So, let's get to work!

Anchoring Success Inside of Yourself

Step 1: The Habit You Broke

Think of a simple nagging habit that you have struggled with that you don't do anymore. Perhaps it was biting your fingernails, not exercising regularly, eating more then you were comfortable with, isolating and not socializing as much as you might like, procrastinating...the list goes on. Identify a time when you decided to shift gears and did so successfully.

The habit that I broke: _____

_____

What I did to successfully accomplish it: _____

_____

_____

_____

_____

How I felt as a result of quitting successfully: _____

_____

_____

_____

_____

Step 2: Visualizing Success

Close your eyes and prepare as you normally would for your visualization practice (if you need a refresher, refer to Beginning to Cultivate an Effective Visualization Practice in chapter 1). Remembering your success in stopping a nagging habit, exclusively focus on the feelings you just wrote down as a result of your success. If your mind drifts elsewhere, gently bring it back to those successful feelings inside. Stay with them for a minute or two. Notice where they live inside of your body. What does the sensation in your body feel like? Tingly, warm, calm? Gently breathe into these feelings of success as you allow yourself to reconnect with them and internalize them. We want to "grow" the experience of these feelings until they become a familiar staple of your daily life. Stay with these sensations for five minutes.

Step 3: Drawing Your Success

Continuing the process, use colored pencils or crayons and draw your "anchored" feelings of success onto the diagram on the following page (figure 1), illuminating each area that you identified in step 2 with a vibrant color of your choice. If you are so inclined, embellish your drawing in a way that really pops. Keep this in mind as a touchstone and template for where you are going. Make this drawing look amazing!

Identifying simple habits that you committed yourself to changing opens the doorway to important resources that *already exist within you*. These same internal resources are essential in changing your relationship with addiction. Of course, changing these practical and mundane habits are much easier to change than addictive processes tend to be. We obviously are not comparing apples with apples here; although some minor habits may be driven by underlying anxieties and worry, genuine addictive processes are much more complex. By and large, the emotional waters that run beneath addiction run deep. So, we need to start in the shallow end of the pool.

Unlike the simple habits that you have successfully overcome, addiction requires attending to something deeper, something more challenging. The practical skills you just identified are great resources to use to change your relationship to addiction. However, they are not sufficient on their own. To find the way through addiction we must find our way to its origins. What has addiction been attempting to self-medicate in the first place?

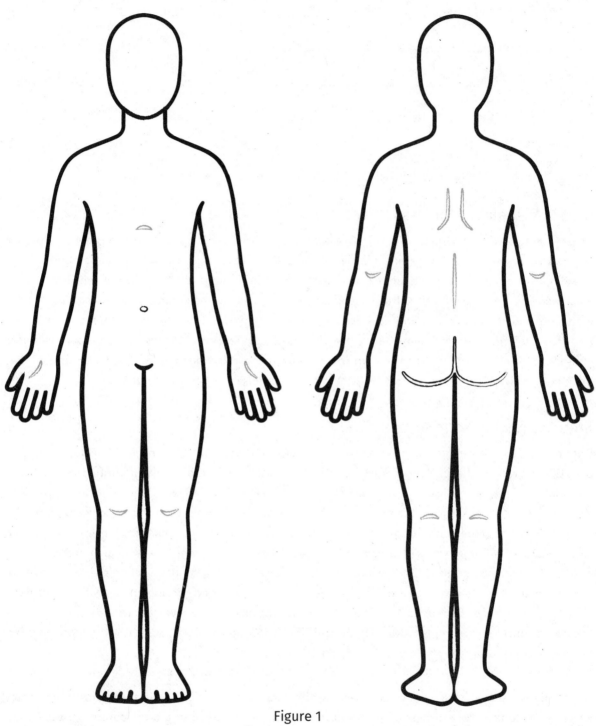

Figure 1

This is where attachment comes into play: we can literally create and utilize healthy, loving relationships that heal the deepest wounds we carry through life so that we won't need to rely on addiction to get us through. In the following chapters we'll explore two scenarios that are very relevant to your journey to transform your relationship to addiction. They are two sides of a coin: *attachment resilience* and *dislocation*. Dislocation—or the felt-sense of disconnection from others, community, ourselves, and our purpose—results from the impact of the difficult life situations and circumstances that compose our worlds. When this sense of disconnection pervades our experience, it is usually because the support of loved ones is not an option. Attachment resilience, the other side of the coin, is the antidote that can provide not only hope but deep healing of the wounds that fuel our addiction.

CHAPTER 3

Dislocation: The Driving Force Behind Addiction

Two catastrophes in recent American history—the terrorist attacks on September 11, 2001, and Hurricane Katrina in New Orleans in 2005—offer insight into the incredible power of human connection.

Given the magnitude of what took place on 9/11, it is extraordinary that only 5 percent of New Yorkers in Manhattan experienced post-traumatic stress disorder (Neria et al. 2011). Conversely, approximately 33 percent of the victims of Hurricane Katrina suffered from PTSD (McLaughlin et al. 2011). So, what accounted for these dramatically different outcomes in people's resiliency and quality of mental and emotional health?

New Yorkers in and around the scene of the attack were running away from the Twin Towers toward their own communities, neighborhoods, families, and trusted loved ones. They had an internal felt-sense of where safety and reassurance could be found: *home*. Their bodies instantaneously mobilized and propelled them toward their familiar safe havens. Immediately, community services were made available, and for weeks after, support literally poured into the city to help, hold, treat, and reassure terrified citizens.

Conversely, citizens in New Orleans trapped in the swirling terror of Katrina and her horrific aftermath were instantaneously turned into refugees. They had to flee their homes, neighborhoods, and communities where family, friends, and relatives had resided for generations. History was lost. Traditions gone. Connections shattered. Thousands of people were displaced to other cities because their homes were permanently destroyed in the hurricane. Unlike New York, there was *no home* to flee to.

These events, although dramatic, provide straightforward examples that help us clarify the most effective, healing, and reliable resources we have for coping with overwhelming life circumstances and painful emotional events. When the shit hits the fan, all we really have is each other. We have the *safe havens* and *secure base* of friends, family, and home—or we feel displaced, isolated, and alone when having to face danger and uncertainty. I am sure that you can guess which group of people would be more susceptible to turning to addictive processes to cope with their respective tragedies.

Write down a few of your thoughts about what personally resonates from these two dramatically different stories of catastrophe, trauma, and resilience.

Dislocation

One of the most overwhelming and impactful hardships we may endure is the experience of dislocation. Dislocation means *a rupture in safe, secure connections* (Alexander 2008). It occurs on many levels. Extreme dislocation can take place on the heels of a natural disaster like Hurricane Katrina. War can dislocate people from their homes and familiar ways of living life. Dislocation can show up hidden in practical change that takes place slowly over the course of time. For example, our communities and neighborhoods have become increasingly siloed and isolated during the past several decades. Dislocation creates loss: loss of home, community, familiarity, tradition, purpose, place, belonging, and connection.

Dislocation occurs in subtle ways as well. You can live within a community but feel very separate and "othered," feeling alone even while among people. You may very well be familiar with the experience of not fitting in, not belonging. It can happen if you are the only Latinx person in an all-white school. It could happen if you are the only trans employee in a heterodominant work culture.

It can also take place in home sweet home. If there is hostility, violence, ongoing shaming, and criticism at home, you can feel displaced from any safe sense of connection. If you were a latch-key kid, you know dislocation. Dislocation leaves us feeling like there is no place where we can comfortably, predictably, and safely belong. No trusted sense of refuge where we feel seen for who we truly are. No place to drop our anchor when the seas of life get choppy. Dislocation is excruciating.

All of us experience some form of dislocation during our lifetimes. For most people it is short-lived. However, when this experience becomes chronic, we live in a world of alienation and disconnection without relief. Dislocation wreaks havoc on our sense of self. It leaves us questioning our self-worth. Without a place to call home in both a personal sense as well as within community, we become lost in a wash of angst, hardship, and isolation. Under these circumstances, drugs and alcohol unfortunately become an extraordinarily common option.

Identifying Your Spheres of Influence

We live within intersecting concentric circles of relationships and environments that form the fabric of our lives. Each sphere of influence has the potential to be either a powerful resource that uplifts and supports our well-being, or a potent force that deters our growth, happiness, and sense of connection with others and the world. Let's explore the spheres of influence in your own life that may be contributing to a sense of dislocation—and driving the pull to use addictive substances and behaviors.

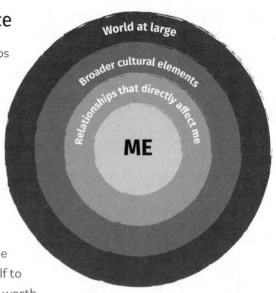

Look at the diagram of concentric circles representing the worlds with which you interact. You are the center of the circle—this is who you are and who you experience yourself to be. Around you are elements that impact your sense of self-worth, lovability, safety, contentment, and hope.

Step 1: Exploring Your Relational World

Below, circle the aspects of your relational world that are most influential and impactful. Write a plus sign (+) next to the circle if it affects you in an uplifting, nurturing way; write a minus sign (−) if it impacts you in a negative, depleting way. There may be other aspects of your immediate life that are important; feel free to add them to the list:

_____   Significant-other relationship

_____   Family, relatives

_____   Work (coworkers, management) or school (teachers, peers, colleagues) relationships

_____   Friends

_____   Neighbors

Other: _____

Other: _____

What is it like to see the number of + and − signs on your list?

_____

_____

_____

Now let's first focus on the aspects to which you attributed a – sign. Name each relational aspect and describe its impact.

Relational Aspect #1: _____

It affects my sense of self-worth and lovability in these ways:

_____

_____

_____

_____

_____

It affects the sense of safety in my life in these ways:

_____

_____

_____

_____

_____

_____

It affects the sense of contentment I experience in my life in these ways:

_____

_____

_____

_____

_____

_____

It affects my sense of hope in these ways:

_____

_____

_____

_____

_____

Relational Aspect #2: _____

It affects my sense of self-worth and lovability in these ways:

_____

_____

_____

_____

It affects the sense of safety in my life in these ways:

_____

_____

_____

_____

_____

It affects the sense of contentment I experience in my life in these ways:

_____

_____

_____

_____

_____

_____

It affects my sense of hope in these ways:

_____

_____

_____

_____

_____

_____

Relational Aspect #3: _____

It affects my sense of self-worth and lovability in these ways:

_____

_____

_____

_____

_____

It affects the sense of safety in my life in these ways:

_____

_____

_____

_____

_____

_____

It affects the sense of contentment I experience in my life in these ways:

_____

_____

_____

_____

_____

_____

It affects my sense of hope in these ways:

_____

_____

_____

_____

_____

_____

There may be additional aspects from this list that you would like to spend time with. If so, that's quite wonderful! It's very commendable that you're allowing yourself dedicated time for self-reflection on your journey to free yourself from addiction.

Step 2: Exploring Your Cultural World

Now let's take a look at the broader cultural world in which you are immersed. This sphere can impart a fantastic sense of pride and belonging, and it can also create the experience of otherness or isolation. Here are a few significant influences within our cultural world that impacts our identities:

- My and my family's socioeconomic status

- Poverty

- My ethnic background and heritage

- My race

- Where I live and the cultural norms there

- My religious affiliation

- My sexual orientation

- My gender identity

- Other: _____

- Other: _____

Explore the cultural aspects of your life in the same way that you worked with your relational ones, by circling those that have been most impactful and then placing + and – signs to indicate how each aspect has affected you. Then explore the negative aspects further by responding to the prompts that follow:

Cultural Aspect #1: _____

It affects my sense of self-worth and lovability in these ways:

_____

_____

_____

_____

_____

_____

It affects the sense of safety in my life in these ways:

_____

_____

_____

_____

_____

_____

It affects the sense of contentment I experience in my life in these ways:

_____

_____

_____

_____

_____

_____

It affects my sense of hope in these ways:

_____

_____

_____

_____

_____

_____

Cultural Aspect #2: _____

It affects my sense of self-worth and lovability in these ways:

_____

_____

_____

_____

_____

It affects the sense of safety in my life in these ways:

_____

_____

_____

_____

_____

It affects the sense of contentment I experience in my life in these ways:

_____

_____

_____

_____

_____

It affects my sense of hope in these ways:

_____

_____

_____

_____

_____

Cultural Aspect #3: _____

It affects my sense of self-worth and lovability in these ways:

_____

_____

_____

_____

_____

It affects the sense of safety in my life in these ways:

_____

_____

_____

_____

_____

It affects the sense of contentment I experience in my life in these ways:

_____

_____

_____

_____

_____

_____

It affects my sense of hope in these ways:

_____

_____

_____

_____

_____

_____

Step 3: Exploring Your World at Large

Life happens—fast and unpredictably. Additionally, *we* change over time. We make life transitions such as moving, changing jobs, dealing with job or housing insecurity, and having to cope with loss or tragedy at times. These changes affect us in dramatic ways that may be out of our control. Here are a few aspects that are part of the bigger picture in the world at large that can affect us deeply:

- The state of the environment

- The state of the economy

- The political landscape

- Public health

- War

- Aging

- Retiring

- Graduating

- Loss of a loved one

- My health

- The changing health of a loved one or friend

- Other: _____

- Other: _____

Circle the aspects of your broader world that have been most impactful. Then place a + or – sign to indicate how each has affected you. Next, explore the negative aspects further by responding to the prompts that follow:

Broader World Aspect #1: _____

It affects my sense of self-worth and lovability in these ways:

_____

_____

_____

_____

_____

It affects the sense of safety in my life in these ways:

_____

_____

_____

_____

_____

It affects the sense of contentment I experience in my life in these ways:

_____

_____

_____

_____

_____

_____

It affects my sense of hope in these ways:

_____

_____

_____

_____

_____

_____

Broader World Aspect #2: _____

It affects my sense of self-worth and lovability in these ways:

_____

_____

_____

_____

_____

It affects the sense of safety in my life in these ways:

_____

_____

_____

_____

_____

It affects the sense of contentment I experience in my life in these ways:

_____

_____

_____

_____

_____

It affects my sense of hope in these ways:

_____

_____

_____

_____

_____

Broader World Aspect #3: _____

It affects my sense of self-worth and lovability in these ways:

_____

_____

_____

_____

_____

_____

It affects the sense of safety in my life in these ways:

_____

_____

_____

_____

_____

_____

It affects the sense of contentment I experience in my life in these ways:

_____

_____

_____

_____

_____

_____

It affects my sense of hope in these ways:

_____

_____

_____

_____

_____

This is extremely deep work which requires your earnest effort and attention. And may stir up the dust in the corners. This is heavy stuff. Please do keep in mind the cliché, "you have to feel it, to heal it." I really commend your courage to wade into the deep end of the pool here. I promise, it really will bear fruit.

To help you learn to tune into your emotional experience and build awareness, now is a good time to do the following exercise. I encourage you to turn to this assessment exercise anytime you are having uncomfortable feelings. The goal is to not turn away from them but to be curious about their intensity, their message, their gift, so to speak.

Your Emotional Thermometer

This is an excellent tool for you to monitor your emotional experience and assist you in learning how to increase your own ability to tolerate your emotions. Your emotional world may be a bit foreign and unfamiliar to you. For most of us, it is a world that has not felt safe or easily accessible to us. You will be able to track when you are in a state of calm and steadiness, when you are feeling mildly uncomfortable, all the way to acknowledging that you may be feeling really stirred up. When you know what you're feeling, you can then seek out other tools and techniques in this book to support you appropriately. Read the scale descriptions and then write down what you feel in this moment. Return to this exercise anytime you need to assess your internal experience.

1 through 3: Cool, calm, and collected. In this state you will notice that you are able to name your feelings, understand them, talk about them, explain what is happening on the inside, and share what your feelings mean to you. In short, you can observe your feelings and understand them without being consumed by them. Oftentimes this experience occurs once you are on the other side of having been immersed in your emotions, having experienced the intensity of your emotions, and then being able to look back on them and understand them from a bit of a working distance. When you have been stirred up emotionally, your goal will be to deliberately bring yourself back to 1 through 3.

4 through 6: Feeling a bit bumpy, but I'm still in the driver's seat. In this state you will be immersed in your emotional experience. You will be feeling your feelings, and it may be a bit intense. However, it is not so intense that you are unable to clearly express what's happening on the inside or make meaning of your experience. You may feel somewhat vulnerable as you become aware that you are reaching into new emotional territory within yourself. You may need to take some time to digest what's going on. We call this *integration*. Integration is a full-brain experience. Your limbic brain (which you'll read about in chapter 5) is active as you viscerally feel your emotions, and your cortical brain is active as it is able to create clear understanding and meaning all at the same time. This is an optimal state for learning and growth.

7 through 10: The ground is shaky under my feet. When the gauge gets beyond 7 you may *not* be able to fully process the emotional experience that is happening. Sometimes the emotion gets so big and unwieldy that the feeling overrides any sense of understanding and meaning. The other side of that coin is suddenly finding yourself shutting down. Numb. This simply means a circuit in the emotional fuse box just blew, and autopilot turned your emotional feeling response off. Either scenario is a clear signal that you may need to slow down, employ some grounding techniques, and take note of what just happened.

Now, sit quietly and assess your emotional temperature in this moment. Jot it down. Then write about how you understand your reading in this moment.

So, what if your emotional temperature is 7 or higher? That means it's time for a grounding exercise, an activity that can bring your awareness to the present moment and return you to the cool, calm, and collected zone. Remember that the higher you rate on the scale, the greater chances of you being either blinded by your emotion or completely numbing out—neither of which is a helpful state in addiction recovery.

In addition to the visualization exercise, Beginning to Cultivate an Effective Visualization Practice, in chapter 1, there are two more exercises—Three-Part Breath and Connect with a Caring Companion—that can serve as tools to assist you in bringing down your emotional temperature. You can also use them throughout the day whenever you want or need to feel more relaxed and present.

Three-Part Breath

This is my favorite tool for grounding. One of the most delightful aspects of the three-part breath is that it is truly a portable practice. You can do it anywhere, anytime. To effectively do the three-part breath:

1. Find a very relaxing place to sit or lie down.

2. Place one hand on your chest and one hand on your abdomen. Simply feel your breath moving up and down.

3. Breathing through your nose, inhale deeply, directing your breath to the floor of your abdomen.

4. Next, inflate the middle part of your lungs (between your abdomen and your chest), and then fill the upper chest completely.

5. As you exhale, do so by beginning your exhalation from the bottom of the diaphragm and emptying the air from your abdomen, then from the midsection of your lungs, and lastly from your upper chest. The exhalation may feel a bit counterintuitive at first. However, with practice it is both enjoyable and enormously relaxing.

6. Do between 5 and 10 repetitions. Then notice how you are feeling on the inside.

The goal is to be able to deliberately calm and soothe the nervous system; this breath is designed to do just that. The more often you do it, the more effective the breath will be in creating a very relaxing sense of calm and peace.

Now that you have tried your first breathing exercise and are hopefully in a calmer state, let's return to your emotional experience. Your next task is to write a narrative of the different forces that you're contending with that may often go unnoticed. Doing so will help you to appreciate how much you have been holding emotionally. My hope is that, as you acknowledge the magnitude and multitude of emotional moving parts that you are attempting to manage, you can be more compassionate with yourself.

_____

_____

_____

_____

_____

_____

Connect with a Caring Companion

It is important to recognize that we can't grieve or process hardship alone. We must do it in relationship. Our greatest resources are each other. That is why this exercise is another important grounding tool that you may want to repeat anytime your emotional temperature is starting to rise.

Now that you have created a clear picture of the forces that you're constantly trying to manage, much like Atlas attempting to carry the world on his back, it is important to consider eliciting the care and support of someone in your life. Ask yourself who would be a safe, supportive, wise, and strong companion with whom you could share the sincere commitment to your growth and recovery. Perhaps you could speak to your significant other, a family member, or dear friend. Perhaps you have a mentor, coach, teacher, or therapist with whom you can share your story. Write down the name of this person and set a date to speak with them.

_____

As you work your way through this book, experiment with what it feels like to share personal parts of your experience and story with another person. This may be a new experience for you, and it takes great courage to be open. Notice what it feels like to take the risk to trust another person with your innermost thoughts and feelings, as well as what it feels like to receive their interests, presence, and support. Record your experiences in a separate section of your journal.

Not all of us have someone who we can confide in at this level, and if that happens to be where you find yourself, that's alright. If that is the case, write a letter to that caring part of yourself that motivated you to read this book in the first place. There is a very significant inner wisdom that has guided you to wanting to redefine your relationship with addiction and live a fuller life. Write the letter to that part of you.

_____

_____

_____

_____

_____

_____

_____

_____

_____

_____

_____

_____

_____

_____

_____

Once you have completed the letter, take a quiet minute of contemplation, and thank yourself deeply for the hard work that you're doing.

You have done a lot of important work in this chapter! I applaud you for making the effort to dig deep and face some fears. Keep in mind that if our distress remains dormant and unattended to, it gains power in the darkness, much like a shadowy secret that never gets revealed. Once we bring challenges and hurt to the healing light of our awareness, we find that we can rapidly create the opportunity to turn a page toward starting a new chapter in our life.

Now that we have explored the depths and realities of dislocation, and the obvious impact on our addictive processes, let's begin to immerse ourselves in the most hopeful part of this entire book: _attachment_. Attachment is the antidote to dislocation. In the next chapter, we will explore how to identify, create, and open channels to powerful attachment processes that genuinely are nature's best medicine for healing pain, a very root of distress that propels addiction into action.

CHAPTER 4

Attachment: Nature's Key to Successful Addiction Recovery

We have a remarkable innate circuitry that has been responsible for our survival and evolution as a species: *attachment*. Human infants require years, even decades, more than any other mammal on the planet to develop the ability to live independently. Compared to other mammals, humans are not endowed with the most power, speed, or ability to camouflage ourselves for protection and survival. Instead, we were given the ability to bond with others, an inherent drive to take care of each other, and a desire to have each other's backs. Attachment is how we successfully navigate and survive the challenges of an unpredictable world.

Eons of evolution has given human infants the ability to communicate what they need and feel directly to their parents *prior to the onset of formal language*. Designated areas within the brain of both parent and child are fine-tuned to accurately translate preverbal (and of course, later, verbal) communication so that we can ensure our infants' health, happiness, safety, and survival.

Parents can differentiate their child's cry that means "I'm scared" from ones that mean "I'm hungry," "I'm tired and need sleep," from "I'm hurt!" This hardwired circuitry enables us to send and receive clear signals that ensure connection with others for survival and perpetuation of the species.

The *quality* and *type* of interactions that routinely occur between caregivers and their young serve another important function: they form the basis of personal meaning. These interactions weave the fabric of the "narratives" we carry inside of ourselves that answer the most fundamental questions of our existence: *Do I matter? Do I hold value? Am I worthy of love and care? Will you be there for me when I need you? Am I safe? Do I belong?*

Attachment interactions form the internal impressions that color our moment-to-moment experience of life. We are not even aware of the influence these daily interactions can have on the quality and meaning of our belief system. They create and determine our inner reality and become the lenses through which we view life. Attachment is powerful.

Attachment theory describes four types of attachment strategies, divided into two categories: *secure* and *insecure*. We'll discuss each type briefly in this chapter. Every person on the planet has an attachment strategy. These strategies were profoundly influenced during crucial moments in our lives when we needed others for support and reassurance and couldn't find it. The repetition of the responses we received during these times formed a template for how we learned to navigate difficulty in our lives.

Interestingly, addictive processes serve the exact same function that attachment strategies offer. They regulate affect, and they attempt to either provide protection or connection. Addiction is so unique as an attachment strategy that it warrants its own category, "The Fifth Strategy," because of its ability to superimpose itself over all attachment strategies. Therefore, no insecure attachment strategy is immune to addiction. It is secure attachment that helps inoculate us from needing to use addictive processes to cope.

Secure Attachment

Secure attachment is the natural birthright of every child. Ideally when our brains expect support, care, and comfort at birth, our caregivers provide it for us. These consistent interactions promote the most optimal and robust development of the brain's neurobiology.

When you were uncomfortable or in distress and reached out, did your caregivers attune to you and respond with warmth and kindness? Did they meet you with love? If you were consistently met with love and support, there is a very high likelihood you are securely attached and well-balanced. That is because in your times of distress, you know how to reach out to others and trust that they will be there for you.

When we are shaken up and consistently responded to with care and support—we accumulate an internal sense of genuinely mattering, belonging, and feeling good about ourselves and others. These experiences become internalized as a strong, positive sense of self. We become resilient. We are imbued with confidence and inner strength, and trust that we won't be alone in our struggles when life is difficult. This is secure attachment.

Sadly, most of us who struggle with addiction did not develop secure attachment. We experienced deep emotional hurt and pain *alone*. And because humans are biologically hardwired to connect, lean in, and receive support and safety in order to dissipate pain and fear, coping alone over the long haul is simply not sustainable. When care does not occur, we often feel down on ourselves. We grow up believing that people will not be there when we need them most. With self-doubt and self-consternation as our baseline experience, in these moments of distress what did we turn to? I think that you already know the answer to this question.

Our attachment experiences are very personal and subjective. Both secure and insecure attachment occur along a continuum. Exploring your experiences will serve as a foundation for further exploration and development of secure attachment to help inoculate you from needing to use addiction as a coping strategy.

Your Experience of Secure Attachment

Take a few minutes to sit quietly and reflect on the most meaningful attachment experiences in your early life. Imagine the warmest memory of your primary caregiver. If you do not have any fond memories of your primary caregiver, try to recall your most cherished caretaker from childhood, be it a grandparent, aunt or uncle, teacher, or coach. How were they there for you? What felt special about the *qualities* of this person or persons? What was it like to be in their presence? How did you feel inside when you were with them? Write down what is coming alive on the inside for you as you reflect on this:

_____

_____

_____

_____

_____

_____

_____

_____

_____

_____

_____

_____

From your personal experiences you are crafting your own definition of secure attachment. These experiences may feel very distant and far away now, but it is encouraging (if you were able to recall a positive memory) that you have had some prior form of secure attachment as a touchstone to build upon.

Or, sadly, you may have drawn a blank. Perhaps you were unable to recall any memories of warmth and responsiveness. I know that this is difficult, but it also begins to affirm why substances have been playing a significant role in your life. There is a very human story that often is overlooked beneath the ongoing struggle with addiction.

Placing Attachment Under a Microscope

Let's build on the previous exercise by placing a finer point on your secure attachment experiences.

1. Recall the positive memories from childhood that you conjured in the previous exercise. Then, circle all the descriptive words below that most resonate with your personal experience.

Safe	Attentive	Embracing
Warmth	Strong	Trusting
Protected	Dependable	Trustworthy
Closeness	Loving	Giving
Attuned	Caring	Inviting
Present	Protective	Inspiring
Available	Supportive	Encouraging
Loved	Responsive	Connected
Lovable	Engaged	Bonded
Predictable	Playful	Harmony
Support	Empathetic	Believed in
Nurtured	Sensitive	Important
Seen	Interested	Carefree
Known	Inclusive	Cared for
Understood	Curious	Held
Reassured	Dialed in	Desired
Comfort	Joyful	Validated
Valued	Friendly	Responded to
Present	Consistent	Matters

2. As you looked back on your life from this perspective, you may have touched upon qualities and feelings that would have been wonderful to have. These qualities might have paved the way for a brighter life—had they been there. Place a star next to the terms that most activate a longing in your heart for what went missing in your attachment experiences.

3. Move into visualization mode (if you need a refresher, see chapter 1).

    Immerse yourself in the thoughts, feelings, and expanded descriptions from steps 1 and 2 above, and imagine a world in which the interactions that you had with others throughout your life (parents, significant others, family, friends, and so forth) were consistently imbued with these qualities. Imagine how things would be if these qualities permeated your entire life both internally (feelings inside of yourself) and externally (with others and the world) to the point that this was your consistent experience.

    Allow this reflection to become a visualization in your mind. The clearer the images, the better. Stay with the images long enough to actually feel what loving attachment feels like inside. Also, pay attention to any emotions that surface as you immerse yourself in this experience. Allow yourself to savor the experience and take as long as you like. Repeat this exercise daily for the upcoming week. Allow it to anchor itself inside of you.

4. Every day for the next seven days, journal about your experience of your attachment visualization.

    Day 1 _____

    _____

    _____

    _____

    _____

    _____

    Day 2 _____

    _____

    _____

    _____

    _____

    _____

    Day 3 _____

    _____

    _____

    _____

    _____

Day 4 _____

_____

_____

_____

_____

_____

Day 5 _____

_____

_____

_____

_____

_____

Day 6 _____

_____

_____

_____

_____

_____

Day 7 _____

_____

_____

_____

_____

_____

In this exercise, you have been painting a picture of the secure attachment that your brain expected at birth. The more detailed your journaling, the more attachment words you identified, and the clearer the visualization you pictured, the more complete your portrait of secure attachment will be. This is our *intended* baseline. This was meant to be our birthright.

The experiences we internalize from these rich and loving interactions become powerful inner resources for us to navigate life when it gets bumpy. These essential qualities are not something that we luckily stumble upon, nor are they something that we can create on our own. They are created through relationship. When they are a staple in our daily lives, they take root inside of us and become the source of powerful inner strength that helps us navigate life's ups and downs. These repetitive positive interactions from these loving people in our lives literally take up residence inside of us.

Reflect on Your Attachment Deficits

Review the qualities that you placed a star next to in step 2 of the previous exercise. These were the qualities that were missing from your life that would have really made a difference had you received them. Reflect upon how your life may have been different had these qualities been consistently present. Complete the prompts, being as detailed, thoughtful, and specific as possible.

If these qualities had been consistently present in my life...

...my self-esteem, or how I see myself, might be different in these ways:

_____

_____

_____

_____

_____

...how I feel seen by others might be different in these ways:

_____

_____

_____

_____

_____

_____

...the way I attain my personal accomplishments, goals, and aspirations might be different in these ways:

_____

_____

_____

_____

_____

...my personal values and ability to uphold them might be different in these ways:

_____

_____

_____

_____

_____

...my capacity for joy, happiness, and contentment might be different in these ways:

_____

_____

_____

_____

_____

...the quality of my relationships might be different in these ways:

_____

_____

_____

_____

_____

_____

Allowing yourself to open the tightly closed gateways that protected you from the pain beneath your addictive processes is quite commendable. If lasting change is what you're after, you are well on your way. This is hard and noble work. Take a moment to acknowledge yourself.

Insecure Attachment

In the absence of the consistent love and support that fosters secure attachment and well-being, we had to adapt to the challenging realities of the world we found ourselves in. We had to make the most of very difficult situations. Quite frequently this meant prioritizing protection over connection.

Based on consistent interactions between caregiver and child, which become the norm, it was discovered that by the time infants are _one year old_, they have already learned whether people would be there for them when they need them..._or not_ (Cassidy et al. 2013; Salter Ainsworth et al. 2015).

When you were uncomfortable or in distress and reached out, did your caregivers neglect you? Did they respond with annoyance and anger? Were you frightened or alone? If so, then reaching out in times of emotional vulnerability would have been daunting. In this scenario, you may have found that no one was there, or that you were a burden, or worse, that you were in harm's way. Therefore, you had to come up with alternate strategies to find a sense of belonging, connection, protection, and self-esteem to experience some semblance of feeling _human_. You would have had to find alternative ways to get the care, attention, and love you needed, or alternatively, to avoid the harm and fear that was ever-present. All of us have had to make some modifications to get our core needs met.

For some of us, our signals of need were never received. We didn't have consistently healthy bonds with caregivers. We were stuck—and maybe continue to be stuck—in a no-man's land for our emotional survival and well-being. This is _insecure attachment_.

"Insecure" is not a judgment, the label simply acknowledges that these strategies are created through difficult life circumstances in which caring, supportive others were not available to us when we needed them throughout our lives. Insecure strategies make perfect sense once we understand what we were needing to adapt to in our early lives. Insecure strategies are not inherently bad—they are simply *ineffective*. They don't get us what we really need.

Your Attachment Environment

This exercise is sensitive and may be challenging. It may touch some of your emotional raw spots, so take your time and be gentle with yourself. Only complete what feels productive for you. And remember that leaning into this pain places you farther along the path to healing from addiction.

1.   Review the list of words that follow. These words are distinctly different from the prior list. They describe the challenging qualities of unhealthy caregiving environments and the emotional obstacles you may have had to navigate. These are also terms that directly influenced the way that you feel about yourself and others, and shaped the way that you interact with people. Circle the words that reflect your early life:

Dangerous	Emotionally cold	Exposed
Distant	Invasive	Absent
Alone	Disliked	Unworthy
Unpredictable	Ignored	Deprived
Invisible	No one listened	Misunderstood
Invalidated	Irritated	Devalued
Absent	Dismissive	Weak
Violent	Scary	Intimidating
Undependable	Irrelevant	Uncaring
Disdaining	Addicted	Volatile
Neglecting	Unpredictable	Mentally ill
Incarcerated	Insensitive	Disinterested
Excluding	Mean	Unfriendly
Inconsistent	Disregarding	Untrustworthy

Self-absorbed	Demoralizing	Discord
Fighting	Arguing	Yelling and screaming
Unimportant	Never believed in	Stressed out
Anxious	Shut down	Unfaithful
Cruel	Terrified	Numb
Judgmental	Condescending	Shaming
Mad	Sad	Desperate
Empty	Hopeless	Powerless
Helpless	Victimized	Ashamed
Shamed	Terrified	Numb

2. Check your internal experience. This exercise may have stirred up some of the dust in the corners of your earliest memories. If so, now would be a great time to take your emotional temperature (see chapter 3) and, if need be, find a quiet place to immerse yourself in the Three-Part Breath exercise (also in chapter 3).

3. Once you are feeling calm and supported, can you try to explore this further? Although this step can be challenging, entering this part of your inner world is the gateway to finally healing the heart of what has been driving your addiction. Select the three most impactful words that you circled. Notice the specific memories connected to each of the three words and name a memory or two associated with each one.

Word 1: _____

Memory: _____

_____

_____

_____

_____

Word 2: _____

Memory: _____

_____

_____

_____

_____

Word 3: _____

Memory: _____

_____

_____

_____

_____

4. Write down what you notice happening inside of you as you take these headlines in:

_____

_____

_____

_____

5. Identify the main theme that you are taking from this exercise:

_____

_____

_____

_____

6. With no one to reliably turn to, using to cope with chronic distress is an understandable (and common) "adaptive strategy." In what ways did your addiction fill the void of secure attachment when you experienced the distress you just identified?

_____

_____

_____

_____

You have been doing the very hard work of identifying the *adaptive function* that your addiction has served all these years. You may be seeing now that when secure attachment is not an option, substances can play an integral role as a surrogate. The problem with addiction is that it takes on a life of its own. Understanding what your addictive process has been attempting to self-medicate offers you awareness, information, and the potential for healthy relational options to help cope with the pain.

Fear and Avoidance in Attachment

Let's examine attachment strategies through the lenses of fear and avoidance. As we discussed, secure strategies are *effective*: they create a sense of connection, understanding, and belonging. Insecure strategies are *ineffective*. They do not foster closeness and support. Instead, these strategies create alienation, confusion, and disconnection. There are three types of insecure strategies—*anxious*, *dismissive*, and *fearful-avoidant*—in which fear and avoidance play a significant role. Therefore, it's not surprising that when we apply the insecure strategies that we learned from our early family relationships to the relationships we currently have in our lives, we find that they get in the way of fostering warmth, support, and connection.

Avoidance in relationships can look like this: When vulnerable, distressing, or conflictual experiences and interactions come our way, we choose to avoid the conflict, avoid rocking the boat, shut down, and even avoid taking important risks in life out of our fear of failure, and at times even fear of success.

We also avoid our own emotional experience to the point of not even understanding what we feel or how to talk about it. This places us at an enormous disadvantage when it comes to receiving closeness and support in life. Without understanding our feelings, we aren't able to understand what we need. And if we can't understand what we feel and need, we literally cannot reach out to others when we need them the most. Therefore, having an attachment strategy high in avoidance means a greater likelihood of becoming even more isolated, leaving us more susceptible to reaching for drugs and alcohol when the going gets tough.

Fear in relationships plays out a bit differently. When our inner worlds are filled with fear, worry, and anxiety, it doesn't take much to place us on shaky ground. Even though a conflict, argument, or tough situation may have happened quite a while ago, it can be difficult for us to shake free of the tension and negativity afterward.

Additionally, the presence of underlying fear and insecurity in our relationships permeates our broader world, often creating high levels of discomfort and agitation elsewhere. When these feelings are our baseline, we easily become more vulnerable to using drugs and alcohol to take the edge off our ongoing inner distress. In tense relational moments there is a greater tendency to blow up, become highly emotional, accusatory, demanding, and loud, pushing our partners away during our crucial times of need.

My Attachment Strategy

Ready to find out your attachment strategy? Below is a list of phrases that describe characteristics of each of the four attachment strategies we use with significant people in our lives. For each strategy, circle the phrases that you most identify with in your close and intimate relationships.

Strategy 1: Low Fear and Low Avoidance

Is happy independently as well as within relationship

Knows that support will be there when it's needed

Trusts that turning to caring others in times of distress is viable

Interacts directly and clearly in times of vulnerability

Has a clear sense of self and other

Is able to see the whole person, strengths as well as limitations

Easily trusts others and can be trusted

Easily accepts love and becomes close

Interdependent in partnerships

Is able to be aware of their emotional world

Expresses emotions in a clear and balanced way

Facilitates repair when there has been conflict

Strategy 2: Low Fear and High Avoidance

Is highly self-sufficient

Views vulnerability as a weakness

Has difficulty allowing genuine closeness

Avoids showing feelings

Is turned off by the display of feelings

Dismisses the need for relationships

Gets annoyed and irritated when partners get too close

Shuts down and distances when vulnerable

Goes numb when in distress or in conflict with partners

Cannot easily identify emotional experience in words

Criticizes partners emotional responses

Feels suffocated in relationships

Strategy 3: High Fear and Low Avoidance

Has low sense of self-worth

Expresses clingy behavior in relationships

Doesn't feel deserving of love and devotion

Is insecure in relationships

Is highly vigilant of criticism and rejection

Lacks ability to let go of negative, conflictual moments

Overly fixates on a worry, concern, or perceived problem

Is reactively irritable

Unnecessarily creates conflict

Is emotionally needy

Is emotionally reactive: criticizes, blames, accuses

Obsessively seeks support and validation from partners

Strategy 4: High Fear and High Avoidance

Has low view of self and can't trust others

Has difficulty being close yet often overwhelmed by isolation

Has difficulty feeling secure in relationships

Has elevated anxiety and fear

Has difficulty regulating emotions especially in relationships

Has history of tumultuous relationships

Feels a deep sense of shame

Is emotionally volatile

Has experienced episodes of self-harming behaviors

Vacillates between idealizing and vilifying people in close relationship

Engages in impulsive and risky behaviors

Experiences episodes of suicidal ideation

Write down the number of items that you circled from each block:

Strategy 1: _____

Strategy 2: _____

Strategy 3: _____

Strategy 4: _____

Notice which block had the most circles. Now let's use the key to uncover your default attachment strategy.

Strategy 1: If most of the sentences that you circled were in strategy 1, then you identified *secure attachment*. Secure attachment strategies score *low on both avoidance and fear* in our primary relationships. Here is what low avoidance looks like: expressing direct, clear communication of feelings and needs to the important people in our lives; inherently trusting that people will consistently respond to us with care; and knowing that it is safe to reach out for care, comfort, and connection. Therefore, there is no need to utilize avoidance as a primary interpersonal strategy. Emotionally safe relationships are the definition of a lack of fear. If you skip ahead to the visuals that follow, you'll see that secure attachment is low on fear and low on avoidance.

Strategy 2: If most of the sentences you circled were in strategy 2, then you likely have an *avoidant attachment* strategy. Avoidant attachment is *low on fear and high on avoidance*. Quite the opposite of anxious strategies, avoidant attachment is organized around deactivation of our emotions and our nervous system. The early emotional environments associated with avoidant attachment are caregivers who were not emotional, not available, and not attuned to our emotional needs. In worst-case scenarios, these strategies were created because of neglect. Therefore, we learned to deactivate our need for relationship, because it was more painful to reach out and find no response than to not reach out at all and maintain some hope that someday someone would be there for us. Being close and connected just doesn't make sense. So, we stay in our own lane and wall off relationships. Shutting people out and turning off our emotions may protect us from further hurt. However, it also prevents us from being able to identify or understand our own emotions, leaving us unaware of what we feel or need.

Strategy 3: This strategy is indicative of *anxious attachment*. Anxious attachment is *low on avoidance and high on fear.* If this is the case for you, then perhaps your experience lends itself to reactivity, emotional volatility, rumination, and high levels of insecurity. Anxious attachment is associated with hyperactivation of our nervous system and our affective processes. This strategy comes out of our needs being intermittently attended to by caregivers, leaving us vigilant with anxious anticipation of whether our needs would be met…or not. We had to keep our relationships in the crosshairs and become reactive and shake things up to make sure we are seen, in hopes of increasing the likelihood of getting on people's radar. Sadly, our style often backfires and pushes people away instead.

Strategy 4: If most of your circles were in this strategy, you likely employ a *fearful-avoidant strategy.* Fearful-avoidant strategies are *high in both fear and avoidance*. They are not only complex, but also highly associated with family environments filled with fear; there is a correlation between having experienced abuse and fearful-avoidant strategies (Erozkan 2016). In moments of distress when the alarm goes off inside of us and our attachment system is activated, the natural tendency is to reach out for comfort, care, and connection. However, if the people we are inclined to reach out to are scary or harmful, then we find ourselves in a horrific bind. Closeness, which all of us need, becomes terrifying. So, we push people away and keep our armor on, only to leave us feeling isolated and alone with our pain. Neither approaching people nor avoiding people feels safe or comfortable. Sadly, both closeness and distance become intensely distressing.

Plotting Your Attachment Strategy

Now let's plot your attachment strategy on the following graph adapted from Dale Griffin and Kim Bartholomew (Griffin and Bartholomew 1994). Keep in mind that *positive view of self* includes feeling a sense of worthiness, of holding value for being who you are, feeling deserving of love, and believing that you are an intrinsically good person. *Negative view of self* conveys the exact opposite: low self-worth, not believing you really hold value, not believing in yourself, and not believing that you are deserving of love, belonging, and connection.

Positive view of other means that you trust others will be there for you when you need them. You see other people, especially significant others, as being inherently good. You have an innate sense that people are interested in you, your life, and your feelings. Conversely, a *negative view of others* conveys the sense that people will not be there for you when you need them. They may receive you with disdain, disinterest, judgment, or worse.

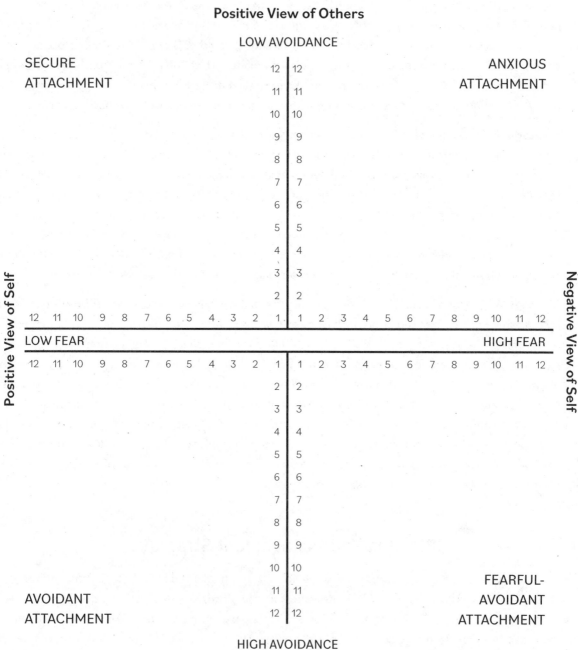

1. Identify the strategy that has the greatest number of descriptions that you circled.

2. Combining the phrases that you circled with the information on fear and avoidance, plot where you land on the graph. Do this by first locating the quadrant for your attachment strategy. Then count the number that you circled and plot it evenly along the numbers for both the X and Y axes on that quadrant.

3. Notice that the graph highlights not only fear and avoidance, but also how fear and avoidance combine to influence whether or not we have a positive view of ourself and others, especially significant others.

4. As you examine where you plot your point on the graph, note how that quadrant pertains to how you most likely view yourself and others. Write down how the formation of your strategy was influenced by your early caregiving environment relative to these beliefs.

_____

_____

_____

_____

_____

_____

_____

_____

_____

_____

5. Pause to reflect. Plotting your attachment strategy can be illuminating in challenging ways. Remember that there are no good or bad attachment strategies. There are only effective or ineffective ones. We are all doing the best we can with what we have.

6. Take a few minutes to write about how learning about your attachment strategy is sitting with you. What holes has addiction filled that were left by your childhood experiences? How did addiction serve your needs in the past and how is it failing you now? Which core needs aren't being met now? Which of them need to be met by loved ones today to make a meaningful change in your addictive behaviors?

_____

_____

_____

_____

_____

_____

_____

_____

_____

_____

_____

_____

By completing this chapter, you have made tremendous progress. You have told a story—your story, emotionally speaking, of what it has been like to walk a mile in your shoes within the most important relationships of your life. For most of us struggling with addiction, this has not been an easy story. However, you are most likely beginning to gain a clear, coherent understanding of how and why addiction took hold in your life. Nice job!

CHAPTER 5

Cues: Our Emotion Activators

As you learned in the previous chapter, attachment is the most basic and reliable source of protection, reassurance, and support for navigating the trials and tribulations of life (Johnson 2005). Our most natural source of protection is relational. Regrettably, leaning on others in times of distress is not an option for everyone. In its place, an internal subconscious process emerges to stand in as a protective firewall against hurt and pain. Without this protective firewall, many of us would not have been able to withstand the debilitating impact of the emotional distress we had to endure. This firewall has a very familiar name: denial.

Denial is linked with a very powerful internal process: compartmentalization. Enduring and managing painful emotional experiences on our own without the opportunity to process and release them through relationship creates a powerful dilemma. Although the firewall effectively protects us from pain, it also compartmentalizes it *inside of us*. We don't get rid of it; we are simply buffered from it temporarily. In time, our distress becomes hidden so well within our neural networks that we aren't even aware of its existence.

Compartmentalization creates a persistent flow of agitation and shame beneath the surface. This "material" becomes a gravitational force compelling us to self-medicate with addiction for relief. In time, we may not even know exactly why we are self-medicating anymore. Ironically, our solution becomes the problem. Keeping the lid on the box requires perpetual use of our drugs of choice, placing addiction in the driver's seat and relegating us to becoming passengers in the story of our own lives.

This chapter is devoted to helping you use the powerful tool of your own awareness so that you can have choice in how you manage your compartmentalized pain before addictive processes take the steering wheel and do it for you. You'll learn about the four components of emotion, and then we'll go deeper into unpacking the first component: our emotional cues. You'll then look at how these cues relate to your addiction.

The Four Components of Emotion

Awareness, specifically emotional awareness, is a powerful resource for transforming your relationship to addiction. When emotions propelling addiction remain invisible, we are rendered powerless to create change. We cannot change that which we cannot see. Therefore, it is essential to access and identify the emotions that we have stored away throughout the years if we want to free ourselves from addiction.

Our emotional hardware is stored within the limbic brain and has been carefully designed to function as an internal alarm system. This part of the brain scans the environment for potential threats to our lives so that we can respond to danger in a moment's notice.

The limbic system responsible for our emotional experience serves as our sentinel at the gate. Emotion is always scanning for safety or danger. Once it determines which of the two it has detected, emotion then signals the rest of our brain and body into action. If we are safe, emotion signals us to remain relaxed and engaged to enjoy the moment. It signals that the coast is clear and that we do not have to expend any energy on vigilance or action. When danger is detected, it signals a fight-or-flight response for survival. This is our emotional system in action. It is profoundly effective and has helped our species survive for thousands of years of life on this planet while facing unfathomable dangers.

Our Emotional Sequence

Emotion is a very high-level processing system designed to direct us toward protection, connection, and healthy social engagement. Emotion is composed of four basic components: the *cue*, the *inner narrative*, *feelings*, and *action tendencies*. Each component provides a unique doorway to access our internal experience.

A **cue** is what activates the emotional system. Our limbic brain notices something has suddenly changed. If it detects that the change is potentially dangerous and we need to act immediately without any abstract cognitive processing, the limbic system activates a very specific emotional signal: fear. It signals the brain to activate multiple domains of functioning as a rapid response system. This is the basis for fight or flight.

Next, our cortex kicks in and rapidly analyzes the situation to accurately identify what is occurring. This analysis takes shape as an *inner narrative* made of words, self-talk, and ideas that create a storyline about the situation. The analysis draws upon information from all of our previous life experiences stored in our brain's "data bank."

In moments of vulnerability and danger, our inner narrative includes deeply personal meanings regarding our sense of adequacy, personal value, and belonging. These narratives prompt waves of *feelings* intended to ready us for action. Feelings are visceral and *embodied*, meaning we feel them physically. Because emotions come from the limbic system, which does not think (thought is generated in the cortex), body sensations (like a racing heart, rapid breathing, tension, and tightness) are the language of emotions (Watson 2023). We feel emotion physically. The more awareness we can bring to understanding our emotional states, the more readily we can find healthy ways of responding to our internal emotional experiences and subsequent needs.

Our narratives and feelings reside in our internal, subjective experience. This makes them difficult to access and identify, yet they happen to be the driving force of our emotional experience. Identifying our compartmentalized narratives and feelings that activate addiction is the key to ultimately attending to the needs embedded in these feelings in a healthy way—without habitually turning to substances.

When narratives become louder and more pronounced, they generate intense feelings inside of us. These feelings activate the end point of emotion: *action tendencies*. Action tendencies are either *approach behaviors* or *avoidance behaviors.* They are determined through biology for our survival: we approach that which is life-giving and avoid that which is life-threatening. Although action tendencies are the most visible component of emotion (along with cues), they may fail miserably at communicating the internal story we have been experiencing.

To get a better sense of how the sequence works, let's explore the following two-episode miniseries:

Episode 1: *Rumaldo returned home during a severe thunderstorm. The power was out, and it was pouring rain outside. Inside, the house was pitch black. While inching his way through the darkness to find a flashlight, he heard a stirring...footsteps from another room... Someone was in the house... In terror, his heart began beating so hard he thought that his chest was about to explode. As he prepared to either fight the intruder or run for his life, the lights suddenly popped on.*

Episode 2: *Instead of a menacing person appearing, Rumaldo saw his partner standing there, equally frightened. They both heaved sighs of relief and warmly embraced one another in a reassuring hug. The threat was over. They made eye contact and noticed that they were both much calmer. Then the two of them burst out laughing.*

Exercise: Identifying the Emotional Structure of the Story

Reread the previous two-episode anecdote and then respond to the questions.

Episode 1

Can you identify the cue that set the entire situation in motion?

Cue: _____

Next, identify the inner narrative primed by the cue. What was Rumaldo telling himself in that moment?

Inner narrative: _____

_____

_____

_____

Although there were not any feelings specifically mentioned, what feelings would most likely be stirred up by the cue and narrative?

Feelings: _____

_____

_____

_____

What possible body sensations (closely associated with feelings) might he have felt?

_____

_____

_____

And finally, the cue, inner narrative, feeling, and body sensations primed the action tendencies. But before we get to episode 2, what *could have been* the possible reactions primed by this ominous experience?

Action tendencies: _____

_____

_____

_____

Congratulations! You have just identified and sequenced the structure of emotional processing that began with hearing a stirring in the darkness to a behavior that was connected to the narrative and feelings generated by the stirring itself.

Now let's explore **episode 2** of the story:

Episode 2

At the end of episode 1, the lights pop on. Who did Rumaldo see?

Cue: _____

What did he tell himself?

Inner narrative: _____

_____

_____

_____

What emotions and sensations did he experience?

Feelings and body sensations: _____

_____

_____

_____

And then what did he do?

Action tendencies: _____

_____

_____

_____

Although the cue and the action tendency are visible and obvious, they only convey a fragment of a much deeper story. The other two components—our inner narrative and feelings/body sensations—are invisible because they occur internally.

Similarly, if the only focus of transforming and healing addictive behavior is on the action tendency of using, the driving force beneath our addictive processes will remain unaddressed, unchecked, and in control. We must identify, access, and process the internal narratives and feelings beneath addiction if we are to heal and grow in meaningful ways.

Applying the Four Elements of Emotion to Addiction

Like the tip of an iceberg, action tendencies reside on top of the vast history of experiences we have had in our lives. Rather than a stand-alone behavior, addiction is an action tendency, or an end point of complex internal processes driven by powerful emotional experiences. Much like defusing a bomb before it detonates, accessing and attending to the source of pain at the heart of addiction will offer us new options to cope with that distress.

Our cortex analyzes changes in our surrounding environments. It also tracks internal changes within us such as emotional tension and distress. When distress becomes strong enough, the brain signals us to seek relief and emotion regulation. It sets an action tendency in motion in an attempt to emotionally stabilize our internal experience.

Let's use the exercise above as an example: Initially, when it appeared that an intruder had broken into the house, the inner narrative was dangerous and frightening. The instinct was to use an avoidance behavior. When it became clear that the mysterious sounds (*cue*) in the dark house were actually Rumaldo's partner, the internal self-talk became, "It is my partner, a trusted, familiar, loving person. I am safe, I can relax [*inner narrative*]. I was pretty scared and frightened [*feelings*], but now that I see my partner, I could use a hug [*action tendency: approach behavior social engagement*]."

This is attachment in action; at the end, an approach behavior signaled social engagement: to reach out for reassurance from a loving other. The couple hugged each other and effectively regulated their distress and fear.

Repeated experiences throughout our lives lay down neural pathways that become stored away in our data banks for future use. They determine our habits when we are experiencing fear and vulnerability. If we trust that we can lean in and people will be there to meet us, that becomes our norm. Addiction tricks our finely tuned biology to reach for something that is bad for us.

Addiction hijacks nature's emotional survival system.

After using for long periods of time, the distress that initially set addiction in motion often fades from awareness but still lives inside of us. All that remains is addiction itself. This is what makes addiction cunning, baffling, and powerful. We lose sight of where it came from in the first place, and we struggle to access the source of what sets it in motion today.

The Cues of Addiction

Now that you have had practice identifying the specific mechanisms of emotion, let's begin to explore the hidden world responsible for setting your addictive process in motion.

Taking a moment to reflect and begin *noticing when you use* offers the clearest pathway to identifying cues that set off addiction in your life. Exactly what is going on in these moments? There may be multiple cues occurring at any given time that could set your addictive process in motion.

Here is an example: In the thick of exam week, Miguel spotted his ex-girlfriend with a new partner. Although he had initiated the breakup, and it was quite amicable, the stress of exams combined with a surprising sense of loss was overwhelming him. To his credit, he hadn't used in months. Even though he had been through much worse over the past year, he had maintained a solid recovery through those tough times.

But there was something different this time... Without being aware of it, the combined recent events threw Miguel into the pain, loss, and devastation of his parent's contentious divorce. It happened so long ago that he rarely thought about it. But now it drew him into an emotional undertow he couldn't make sense of—after all, the specific events themselves weren't really all that difficult for him. Yet, his current distress was disproportionate to what was happening in his life. Without awareness of so much unfinished business from long ago, Miguel became swept away in pain that he was unable to identify. His recovery had been solid for close to one year. But being unable to get a handle on what was occurring inside of him, Miguel began using pills again to quiet the pain.

A perfect storm blew into Miguel's life. What happened? Have you ever heard the phrase "under enough stress, we all regress?" Well, the emotional familiarity of loss during a very heightened time of stress had the power to unlock Miguel's compartmentalized hurt and pain from his childhood. The surge of emotion was so strong that, before he knew it, he was using.

The specifics of Miguel's story may be different from your own, but we all have been susceptible to the impact of the perfect storms in our lives. They have often led to falling off the wagon from our recovery.

Identifying Your Addiction Cues

Begin this exercise by reading the category headings and descriptions of the addiction cues that follow. Then read through the list beneath each heading and circle the ones that are most relevant to you. This list is far from exhaustive, and you may add some examples from your own life below.

Discrete events: Powerful specific events that shook you up or profoundly impacted you either in the past or recently, such as an enormous loss or an awful experience. These provide predictable cues for self-medicating with addiction. Here are some cue examples:

- Being in a bad car accident

- Being suddenly fired from your job

- Getting bullied at school

- The death of a loved one

- Relationship breakup

- Divorce

- Sudden illness or injury to yourself or a loved one

- Physical or sexual assault

- _____

- _____

- _____

- _____

Troubling childhood home or family or caregiving environment: Was growing up at home during your formative years painful or traumatizing? What was (or is) the vibe at home? Experiencing the impact of pain and negativity in our most important relationships is one of the most potent negative cues for using. Some cue examples:

- Neglect

- Addiction of a significant other, parent, or sibling

- Mental illness of a significant other, parent, or sibling

- Experiencing or witnessing violence

- Physical, sexual, or emotional abuse

- Chronic parent or family conflict

- _____

- _____

- _____

- _____

Current ongoing circumstances and environments: Are your work, school, or community environments or circumstances toxic, depleting, or demoralizing? When you leave work do you feel disrespected, overlooked, treated poorly? Does your significant-other relationship create harm or distress? Is school somewhere that leaves you feeling isolated or down on yourself? Having to spend large portions of each day in these environments can create a lot of emotional pain and erode your sense of self. This is very fertile ground to cue your addiction. Examples:

- Poverty

- Neglect

- Addiction of a significant other, parent, or sibling

- Being scapegoated

- Really struggling with school and never hitting the mark

- Being the victim of harassment

- Experiencing or witnessing violence

- Physical, sexual, or emotional abuse

- Chronic parent or family conflict

- _____

- _____

- _____

- _____

Disparaging social situations: Are your social groups toxic and triggering to your well-being? Do you feel devalued, ostracized, judged, invisible, or put down? Our social worlds create the fabric of our lives.

Feeling alone, isolated, and less than can readily cue addiction as a quick and easy way to numb the pain. Examples:

- Victim of ongoing physical or cyberbullying

- Picked on by the neighborhood kids

- Constantly being the butt of jokes

- Never being invited to join social gatherings

- _____

- _____

- _____

- _____

Painful emotions from within: Many of us have an inner felt-sense baseline of feeling less than, frightened, ashamed, unimportant, and powerless. These baseline feelings can have a profound effect on our relationship to addiction, and very consistently provide an ongoing cue for us to use. Examples:

- Self-loathing

- Deep hurt, sadness, and depression

- Self-doubt, second-guessing yourself, or feeling like an imposter

- Feeling alone and isolated

- Deep shame and inadequacy

- Uncontrollable fear and anxiety

- _____

- _____

- _____

- _____

Not being true to your core values: We have a genuine sense of what feels right and what feels wrong in the way that we approach and live our lives. Although these values and beliefs may remain unspoken, we usually have a clear sense of when we are living in harmony with them and when we have let ourselves down. This perceived personal failure can be a potent addiction activation cue. Examples:

- Going along with things that you don't believe in

- Not standing up for someone who has been wronged

- Settling for less than you deserve or are capable of achieving

- Avoiding taking risks to go for what you desire

- Not speaking up for yourself

- _____

- _____

- _____

- _____

Negative cultural elements and community influences: Many of us walk into places and spaces within our everyday lives concerned about safety as our first thought. Not everyone is free from worrying about feeling othered, marginalized, or worse. These fears, worries, and concerns are very present and real for so many of us. The constant impact of these realities is also a predictable cue for addiction. Here are a few cue examples:

- Being denied opportunities because of one of your identities

- Being the victim of violence and ridicule because of one of your identities

- Feeling constantly rejected and put down because of one of your identities

- Never feeling a sense of belonging

- Feeling ashamed of who you are due to one or more of the identities you carry

- _____

- _____

- _____

- _____

Return to this exercise throughout the week to explore and expand upon the influences that cue addiction. Give yourself permission to be incredibly curious and devoted to answering this one question: *What is it that sets my addiction in motion?*

To dive deeper into identifying the forces involved in prompting addictive behaviors in your life, track the cutes that set off your addictive process. Use the chart below to get started. You can print copies of this chart to complete each day over the coming week at http://www.newharbinger.com/52403.

CUES THAT SET OFF MY ADDICTIVE PROCESS

Date:	
Cue	
What happened?	
Where did this take place?	
Were other people involved?	
What thoughts (inner narrative) surfaced?	
What feelings surfaced?	
What category(s) do your answers fall into?	

After charting your cues for one week, review your data. Write down your observations and any new awareness that have resulted from this exploration.

_____

_____

_____

_____

_____

_____

_____

_____

What is it like for you to see this mapped out?

_____

_____

_____

_____

How can you use these discoveries of cues to use to increase your awareness of what's been going on inside of you when you feel triggered?

_____

_____

_____

_____

_____

_____

Being able to identify what is underneath the hood when a cue has set your addiction in motion is enormously empowering. You are beginning to use your awareness as a strategic tool to cultivate options other than addiction to help you navigate challenging emotional moments. This is really hard work. Way to go! The next chapter will focus on identifying and processing your inner narratives, then we will explore the feelings that surface from them, as well as the action tendencies that often culminate in using.

CHAPTER 6

Inner Narratives: Our Meaning Makers

In chapter 5, we discussed the inner narrative as one of the four components of our emotions. In this chapter, we'll delve more deeply into the role our inner narrative plays in our addiction. We'll look at the painful and challenging stories that play out internally when your addiction is activated by one of your cues. Identifying your core narrative is the most challenging element of the four parts of your underlying emotional experience.

The negative inner narratives beneath your addiction can be hard to acknowledge. However, by not acknowledging them we pay a huge price. Allowing them to go undetected empowers them to act like a hidden magnet urgently pulling us toward addiction without even knowing why we are doing so. Let's go on a journey to uncover the narratives that are being activated by your cues.

Defining Inner Narratives

Inner narratives are the thoughts, meanings, and stories that get set in motion the moment a cue is triggered. They can help us decode the underlying reasons that we use in the first place. Inner narratives are extraordinarily important access points that guide us into the ever-elusive world of our inner experience. They are extremely subjective, and they vary widely. They narrate the *personal storyline* that lives behind the scenes of addictive behavior.

Unfortunately, stigma and judgment of addiction is still alive and well today. Rather than consider why people might use in the first place, predetermined, often shame-based assumptions are thoughtlessly cast about, wrongly disparaging the personal integrity and moral character of people who struggle with addiction. Often, the focus remains solely on the substance itself. The painful human struggles and the experiences of displacement that led to addiction remain invisible and unacknowledged. This perspective is so woven into the fabric of everyday life that we too may lose sight of our own personal struggles living beneath the surface of addiction.

Inner narratives help us to rediscover the human face, *your* human face, that lives behind addiction. The truths within our narratives reveal crucial information about our inner worlds and offer opportunities for coping with distress in healthier ways.

If we are to really heal our addiction from the inside out, using inner narratives to decode what's been happening under the surface gives us the best possible platform for finally healing the source of addiction in and of itself.

The Stories of Jonas and DeMarcus

As a child and teenager, Jonas was repeatedly assaulted by a member of the clergy in his small town. Most of the townspeople, including his family, were extremely religious. The clergy were the most revered people in the community. Jonas was told that nobody would believe him if he were to seek help for what he had to endure, so he felt that he had no other option but to keep the shameful secret deeply hidden. He kept his pain and shame at bay with alcohol, pills, and pot. After years of using, several DUIs, and several troubled relationships, Jonas got sober.

Recovery became his primary focus. He was deeply committed to it and became extremely successful. Despite what occurred in his early life, his sobriety, and the recovery network he created supported him to successfully accomplish important milestones of life, including a happy marriage.

One day, several years into his marriage to DeMarcus, DeMarcus told Jonas that he wanted to pursue becoming a member of the clergy. Suddenly, seeing the white collar around his partner's neck threw Jonas into a silent, agonizing tailspin. Jonas would never consider revealing anything about the nightmare that was his childhood. And there was no need for anyone to ever ask: given Jonas's cheerful demeanor, years of sobriety, and stable life, no one ever suspected that his early years were filled with trauma, isolation, and abuse. Although the collar was simply part of the required attire of the clergy in DeMarcus's church, it represented a familiar symbol of Jonas's childhood. This symbol unearthed the unfinished business and unprocessed pain of Jonas's past that he had buried deeply inside of himself for years.

Jonas was overcome with fear, anxiety, and irritation. His behavior became very erratic. He was frequently late to work and found himself avoiding both DeMarcus and his friends. This was extremely hurtful and confusing to DeMarcus, who thought that something was horribly wrong, and Jonas was rethinking the marriage.

One day, DeMarcus discovered several empty bottles of vodka hidden in a back corner of the basement. He knew how important Jonas's recovery was to him and had never known Jonas to drink. After much deliberation, DeMarcus confronted him, and they had a long, painful, yet much-needed heart-to-heart conversation.

Jonas leaned in and took an enormous risk with his husband. He shared his story for the very first time. Through tears and sobbing, they began the process of opening the door to Jonas's grief, pain, and abuse of his past. And with the help of DeMarcus and a good therapist, Jonas was able to let go of the past and return to a sober lifestyle.

Now, if you or I had observed our partner wearing the white collar of clergy (other than it being way out of the ordinary for most of us!), that cue would not have even registered as anything remotely troubling, let alone horrific. For Jonas, however, it had a deep, significant, and very specific meaning: it set the most painful internal narratives of his life in motion. He was living with a horror film playing inside of himself. Without understanding the personal and painful internal narrative it evoked, it would have been impossible to understand Jonas's relapse.

Our inner narratives reveal the personal, hidden stories that are unique to our own life history. Therefore, what you see on the surface never tells the whole story when it comes to addiction.

Many of us have used denial and compartmentalization to cope with the pain of the unresolved challenges in our lives. If we have buried the distress from our life histories deeply inside of ourselves, then we remain vulnerable to current moments and situations that feel familiar or similar to our unresolved events. In other words, when our inner narratives remain invisible to us and lurk silently in the shadows of our being, they perpetuate the need for us to continually use addictive processes to keep the lid on the box without us even knowing what we are self-medicating.

The Power of Inner Narratives

In addition to emotion providing us with a finely tuned built-in alarm system capable of sending us lightning-quick safety signals in a moment's notice, it also provides us with the sophisticated ability to make meaning of situations as they occur. Similar to an enormous hard drive, our brain collects and retains data from everything that we have been exposed to and everything that we have learned throughout our entire lives. It uses this information to compare current situations to previous life experiences, so that we can take the most life-giving and danger-avoiding action possible in any given moment.

Once a cue triggers us, our brain instantaneously identifies similar experiences, and applies stored meaning to what is occurring. The stored meanings constitute our inner narratives. This process occurs rapidly and often outside of our conscious awareness. This information dictates whether we need to approach the situation or avoid it (the approach and avoidance behaviors (action tendencies) we discussed in the previous chapter). We all experience objective situations in subjectively unique ways. It is the *meaning* that differs. Becoming aware of these stories is a crucial part of transforming your relationship with addiction. It is through understanding the personal meaning of our narratives that we can accurately interpret the cues and respond to them thoughtfully without moving immediately toward addiction.

And here is a key point: *It is not the cue in and of itself that sets addiction in motion; it's the uniquely personal meaning of the cue and the emotional feelings they stir up that are at the heart of our using.* Identifying our inner narrative empowers us to target the parts of ourselves that have been beckoning for support and healing. Once we understand the meaning of our inner narratives clearly, we can replace our need for addiction with healthy methods for reassurance and peace.

Identifying the Negative Inner Narrative Beneath Addiction

Have you ever asked yourself, *Why is this particular cue so potent for me, while other cues don't seem to affect me at all?* Or, *What is it about this specific cue that really gets to me?* For example, you might be intensely impacted when you let people down and disappoint them; disappointing others routinely ends with you using. However, you have noticed that when your friends let others down, they seem to take it in stride and correct course fairly easily.

Let's explore the inner narratives and meanings behind *your* cues. To begin, flip back to the list of cues that you identified in the previous chapter. Select the three that are the most potent and write them below. Then consider the stories you tell yourself related to that cue. What self-talk comes to mind? Write down what you say to yourself.

Cue #1: _____

When this cue triggers me, this is what I say to myself about…

…my self-esteem and how I see and feel about myself: _____

_____

_____

_____

_____

…how I feel seen and perceived by others: _____

_____

_____

_____

_____

…my ability to attain my personal accomplishments, goals, and aspirations: _____

_____

_____

_____

_____

…showing up in a meaningful way in my relationships: _____

_____

_____

_____

_____

...staying true to my core values: _____

_____

_____

_____

_____

...my capacity for joy, happiness, and contentment: _____

_____

_____

_____

_____

Cue #2: _____

When this cue triggers me, this is what I say to myself about...

...my self-esteem and how I see and feel about myself: _____

_____

_____

_____

_____

...how I feel seen and perceived by others: _____

_____

_____

_____

_____

...my ability to attain my personal accomplishments, goals, and aspirations: _____

_____

_____

_____

_____

...showing up in a meaningful way in my relationships: _____

_____

_____

_____

_____

...staying true to my core values: _____

_____

_____

_____

_____

...my capacity for joy, happiness, and contentment: _____

_____

_____

_____

_____

Cue #3: _____

When this cue triggers me, this is what I say to myself about...

...my self-esteem and how I see and feel about myself: _____

_____

_____

_____

_____

...how I feel seen and perceived by others: _____

_____

_____

_____

_____

...my ability to attain my personal accomplishments, goals, and aspirations: _____

_____

_____

_____

_____

...showing up in a meaningful way in my relationships: _____

_____

_____

_____

_____

...staying true to my core values: _____

_____

_____

_____

_____

...my capacity for joy, happiness, and contentment: _____

_____

_____

_____

_____

Great work! This is a very difficult task, and it is extraordinarily commendable that you risked opening the door to what your addiction has been masking for quite some time. This is a great time to check in with yourself. Take your emotional temperature (see chapter 3). If your emotional temperature is higher than you would like, find a relaxing place to practice the Three-Part Breath exercise (also in chapter 3) for about five minutes.

As you go through the week and you continue to turn your attention inward toward these very elusive narratives, you may find yourself identifying even more of them! That is fantastic news. The more you understand about the moving parts that set your addictive process in motion the more you can intervene on your addiction's momentum before it sabotages your life.

Sharing Your Discoveries with Someone Meaningful

These narratives can be pretty heavy. It's very common to have carried these painful narratives inside of us for most of our lives. Carrying these messages alone can be exhausting and demoralizing. The only thing worse than hurting and being in emotional pain is *hurting alone*.

In chapter 3, you identified a safe, reliable person to whom you could turn. It may have been the very first time that you ever opened up to somebody. When we can feel people caring, being interested in what we go through, and being willing to share the load with us, life gets brighter, our load gets lighter, and we begin to create a solid path for letting go of our addictions.

Seek out this same person, or another safe person in your life, and begin to share more of what you've been carrying on the inside for all these years. Here are some steps to consider.

1. Reach out to set up a time to get together and talk. Let them know that they are important you, that you really trust them, and that you would like to share the fruits of your personal-growth work toward changing your relationship with addiction.

2. When you meet with your person, frame the topic of conversation clearly for them. Let them know that you've been working hard to break free from addiction, and that you would like to confide in them about your recent discoveries. Ask them to simply listen. Encourage them to attune to the details of what you share as well as the emotional sentiment behind your newfound discoveries.

3. Make sure they are aware that you're not seeking advice or asking them to fix anything. Reiterate that you're simply asking them to be there with you as someone in your life who really cares about you, so that you are not holding all this alone.

4. Share your new discoveries from a genuine and heartfelt place.

5. As you speak, notice what thoughts and feelings surface. Notice what their caring response feels like. Notice what it feels like to have risked leaning into another person and sharing the details of your inner world with them.

If you are not able to identify anybody with whom you can speak, you can reference the qualities of the ideal attachment figure that you identified in chapter 4. Quietly visualize a person embodying those qualities as you share with them what you've been discovering. Pay exquisite attention to the look in their eyes, the expression on their face, the tone in their voice, and their way of receiving you as you take this risk to be known.

After you have shared the fruits of your labors and concluded the conversation with your real or virtual person, take some time to write down what it was like to experience leaning into a person who cares about you and sharing what you have been going through.

_____

_____

_____

_____

_____

_____

_____

_____

_____

_____

_____

_____

_____

_____

You have taken enormous steps toward paving a new pathway through addiction. Not only did you do the hard work of rolling up your sleeves and identifying hidden inner narratives, you have taken a risk in sharing them rather than holding them alone. Congratulations for exploring another doorway into your emotional world. You are making excellent progress toward moving yourself into the driver's seat of your life and having more choice over your addictive processes.

In the upcoming chapter, we will identify how our inner narratives gain momentum internally and naturally generate feelings. The subtle combination is a very potent mix. You will discover just how this combination manifests in your life as the stealth driving force under the hood of your addictive process.

CHAPTER 7

Feelings: Our Motivation Fuel

In the previous chapter, we discussed the inner narrative as one of the four components of emotion that exerts a potent influence on our addictive process. In this chapter, we'll delve deeply into what may be the most active *force* beneath addiction: emotional feelings.

Feelings activate our response to the "stories" that our inner narratives carry. Emotions have the power to either propel us away from healthy engagement and reassurance, or they can serve as meaningful resources for connection, growth, and healing—propelling us toward caring engagement with others.

The Power Beneath Choice and Action

The Latin root of emotion is *emovēre*: it means *to move away from*. The visceral experience of emotion literally propels us into action. When we have grown up in securely attached families and get triggered by an intense cue in life's rocky moments, the pain of the situation itself will be accompanied by an additional influence: the inner narratives formed through the countless supportive interactions we have experienced from caregivers throughout our lives. These positive narratives generate an emotional experience. We don't question the availability of help, nor do we question whether we are loved or if we matter. We know it in our bones. *We feel it*. This is an example of our emotions moving us; emotions prompting us to take action. We are automatically propelled to seek reassurance and the support of others in healthy, effective ways. With secure attachment, there is no need to self-medicate distress through addiction.

Conversely, given how deeply important our caregivers were to us, if they were routinely hostile or neglectful, then very personal negative meanings take root inside of us. These experiences eventually become deeply embedded as negative narratives and color our sense of self, our sense of others, and even how we see the world. Sadly, our caregivers' lack of caring responsiveness created the cues for the narratives that define our lives.

Such narratives are far from neutral. Each time they surface they elicit a profound negative emotional experience accompanied by feelings that remind us that others won't be there for us when we need them. The emotions from these moments propel us to take action as well, but in a very different direction. One direction that offers a quick and effective "solution" for numbing hurt and loneliness is addiction. Addiction will dull the pain...temporarily. In this way our attachment history's influence on our inner emotional world is inherently connected to using and addiction.

Here is the good news: none of us is held hostage to our histories. The majority of this wiring occurred when we were quite young and not as wise, experienced, and capable as we are today. As you begin to make more of a connection between the emotional nature of your attachment world and your addictive process, you will begin to understand how and why adapting your circuitry to seek substances at that time in your life was necessary. Understanding your emotional world will provide a pathway for you to identify what was missing and get your needs met in healthy, meaningful ways without reaching for substances.

The Connection Between Emotions and Addiction

If your life circumstances conspired to rob you of the birthright of secure attachment, and you found yourself facing major challenges without the support of dependable loved ones, you have probably been pulling the emotional load alone for an extraordinarily long time. The longer you do it, the heavier the load gets. When the load gets heavy and the inner narrative reinforces that we are alone, unimportant, and don't have a reliable place to go with this pain, our life fills with painful emotions. Feelings prime and activate action tendencies—including addiction.

Exploring and Expanding Your Emotional Vocabulary

This exercise is meant to give you a starting place to develop *emotional fluency*. Emotional fluency is a useful tool for determining precisely what you are experiencing in any given moment. Knowing what you are experiencing emotionally in the moment allows you to access any needs connected with whatever you may be going through.

Refer to the list of the six core emotional feelings and their variations, and answer the prompts that follow. This list is not exhaustive, and the blank spaces are there for you to fill in any others you may think of.

Anger	Sadness	Happiness	Fear	Disgust	Shame
Annoyed	Heartbroken	Joyful	Frightened	Horrified	Embarrassed
Furious	Forlorn	Elated	Terrified	Grossed out	Worthless
Irritated	Unhappy	Psyched	Shaken up	Repulsed	Despised
Rageful	Tearful	Cheerful	Anxious	Sickened	Not valued
Pissed off	Down	Glad	Shaky	Appalled	Lowly
Hateful	Despair	Ecstatic	Freaked out	Offended	Unlovable
Resentful	Upset	Delighted	Alarmed	Outraged	Unwanted
Ticked off	Depressed	Uplifted	Panicked	Nauseated	Humiliated
Bitter	Melancholy	Blissful	Dread		Unimportant
Aggravated	Disheartened	Thrilled	Worried		Don't matter
Exasperated	Grief	Overjoyed	Afraid		Irrelevant
Outraged	Joyless	Stoked	Scared		Despicable

Tender, Supportive Emotional Feelings

Return to the exercise "Placing Attachment Under a Microscope" in chapter 4. Allow yourself to re-experience the words that you circled and the statements that you wrote describing your experience of comfort, care, and connection. Sit with them for a moment. Then, select several words from the chart above that emotionally correspond with your responses from that exercise.

1. _____

2. _____

3. _____

4. _____

5. _____

Write down *why* you just selected these specific words from the chart:

_____

_____

_____

_____

_____

_____

Next, using the diagram, identify where these positive feelings register in your body.

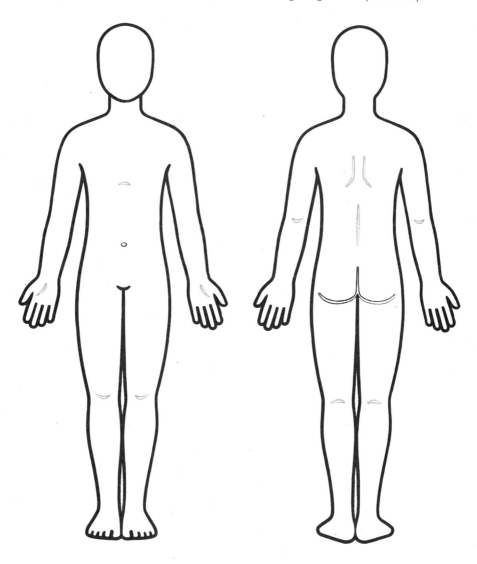

What physical sensations did you notice?

_____

_____

_____

_____

_____

How is it for you to feel positive-feeling sensations physically in your body?

_____

_____

_____

_____

_____

Tough and Challenging Emotional Feelings

By way of contrast, let's dramatically shift gears to explore how you experience the more challenging emotions. Revisit the exercise "Identifying the Negative Inner Narrative Beneath Addiction" in chapter 5. Choose one cue to dig into deeper. Visit http://www.newharbinger.com/52403 to print more copies of this worksheet so you can explore and work with other cues you've identified.

Cue: _____

When this cue triggers me, this is what I say to myself about…

…my self-esteem and how I see and feel about myself: _____

_____

_____

_____

_____

...how I feel seen and perceived by others: _____

_____

_____

_____

_____

...my ability to attain my personal accomplishments, goals, and aspirations: _____

_____

_____

_____

_____

...showing up in a meaningful way in my relationships: _____

_____

_____

_____

_____

...staying true to my core values: _____

_____

_____

_____

_____

...my ability to cope with life's challenges: _____

_____

_____

_____

_____

Read this over carefully. Allow your words touch you. Notice what comes alive inside of you. These difficult inner narratives are profoundly emotional. We tend to numb these feelings and keep them hidden from ourselves. You have probably noticed that they manage to come out sideways later and sabotage your life.

Return to the emotional vocabulary chart and select the feeling words that best describe the emotional reality that you experienced from each category of cue #1. Write down what it is like to connect with these feelings:

My self-esteem and how I see and feel about myself

Feelings:

1. _____

2. _____

3. _____

4. _____

What happens inside of you when you connect these feelings to this part of your narrative?

_____

_____

_____

_____

_____

_____

Which physical sensations accompany these feelings? Place them onto the diagram:

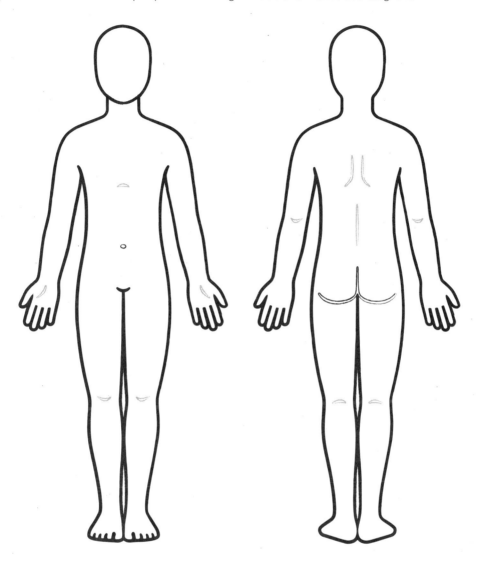

What is it like for you to experience the emotions and body sensations from your narrative?

_____

_____

_____

_____

_____

_____

_____

_____

How I feel seen and perceived by others

Feelings:

1. _____

2. _____

3. _____

4. _____

What happens inside of you when you connect these feelings to this part of your narrative?

_____

_____

_____

_____

_____

Which physical sensations accompany these feelings? Place them onto the diagram:

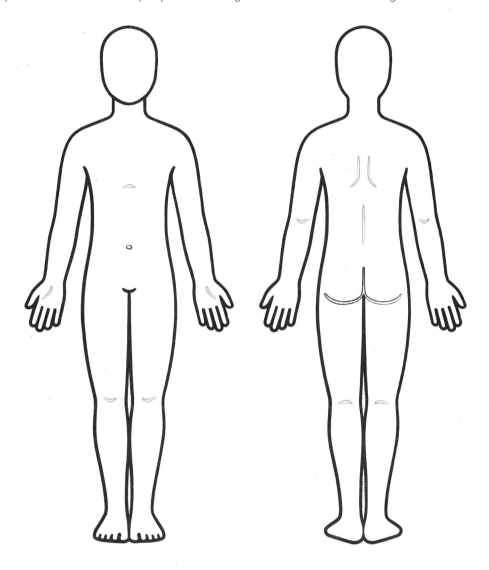

What is it like for you to experience the emotions and body sensations from your narrative?

_____

_____

_____

_____

_____

_____

_____

_____

_____

My ability to attain my personal accomplishments, goals, and aspirations

Feelings:

1. _____

2. _____

3. _____

4. _____

What happens inside of you when you connect these feelings to this part of your narrative?

_____

_____

_____

_____

_____

Which physical sensations accompany these feelings? Place them onto the diagram:

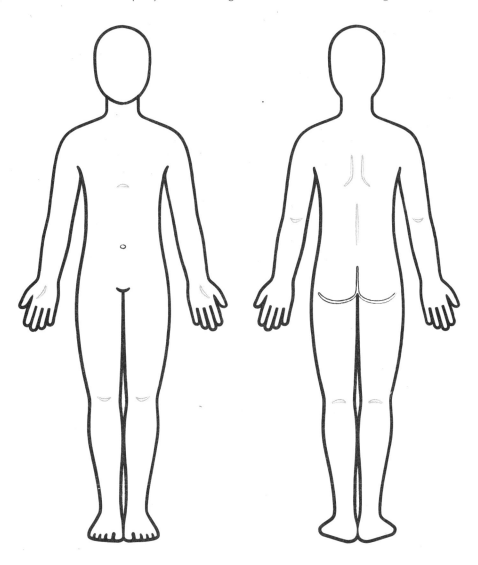

What is it like for you to experience the emotions and body sensations from your narrative?

_____

_____

_____

_____

_____

_____

_____

_____

Showing up in a meaningful way in my relationships

Feelings:

1. _____

2. _____

3. _____

4. _____

What happens inside of you when you connect these feelings to this part of your narrative?

_____

_____

_____

_____

_____

Which physical sensations accompany these feelings? Place them onto the diagram:

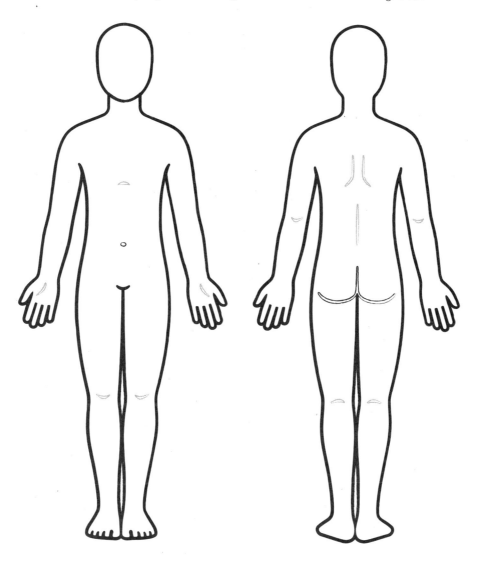

What is it like for you to experience the emotions and body sensations from your narrative?

_____

_____

_____

_____

_____

_____

_____

_____

Staying true to my core values

Feelings:

1. _____

2. _____

3. _____

4. _____

What happens inside of you when you connect these feelings to this part of your narrative?

_____

_____

_____

_____

_____

Which physical sensations accompany these feelings? Place them onto the diagram:

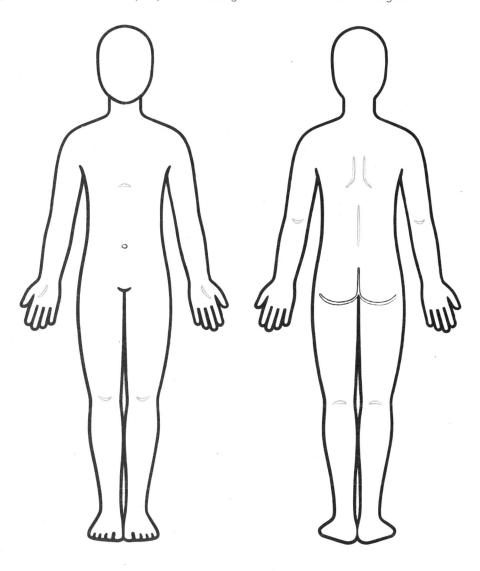

What is it like for you to experience the emotions and body sensations from your narrative?

_____

_____

_____

_____

_____

_____

_____

_____

My ability to cope with life's challenges

Feelings:

1. _____

2. _____

3. _____

4. _____

What happens inside of you when you connect these feelings to this part of your narrative?

_____

_____

_____

_____

_____

Which physical sensations accompany these feelings? Place them onto the diagram:

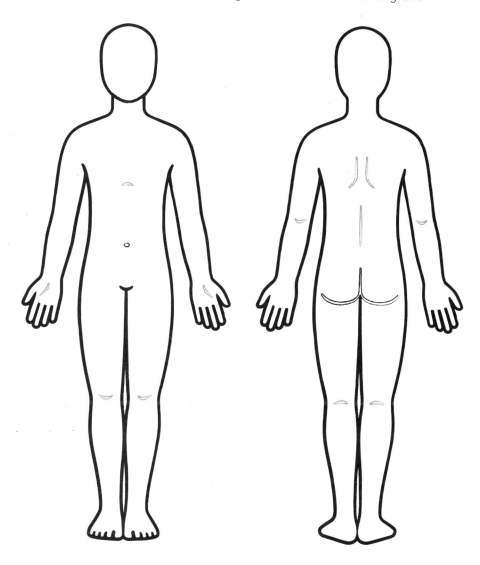

What is it like for you to experience the emotions and body sensations from your narrative?

_____

_____

_____

_____

_____

_____

_____

_____

In previous chapters you connected your painful inner narratives to your most challenging addiction cues. In this chapter, you have successfully taken the process one step further: you've identified and experienced the hidden challenging emotions that get activated each time these narratives cycle through you internally. Now that you are connecting the dots and can see how your addictive behavior is actually the end point of a vast, hidden, and painful set of internal experiences, write about what it is like for you to make these connections about your life and your addictive process.

_____

_____

_____

_____

_____

_____

_____

_____

You have been engaging in the empowering practice of turning your awareness inward and beginning to understand the path that got you caught in the throes of addiction. I hope this helps you to begin seeing yourself from a more humane, compassionate, and caring stance. Your addictive process was not created in a vacuum. It took a lot to get here. You are now on the road to setting yourself free.

You have successfully identified three of the four elements of the emotional process that has been setting your addiction into action: the cue, inner narratives, and emotional feelings. Congratulations! Narratives and emotions are very subtle, and yet they exert enough power to run your life in directions you may not always want it going in. In the next chapter, we will bring to light the fourth and final element of emotion: action tendencies.

CHAPTER 8

Action Tendencies: The Culmination of Emotion

This chapter explores the way that your inner emotional world is either effectively or ineffectively communicated to others through your specific style of communicating, aka your *action tendency*. Emotional experience resides beneath the surface and prompts visible expression above the surface. For example, feelings of sadness often promote crying or reaching out to others to elicit support. Anger may culminate in standing our ground to advocate and protect ourselves. Fear tends to activate fight, flight, or freeze.

Action tendencies represent a very small part of our emotional experience, but because they are so highly visible, they can eclipse our inner experience and be easily misinterpreted. Therefore, the clearer and more direct our communication style, the more likely we will be understood and responded to.

When it comes to attachment and creating connection with people in our lives, action tendencies are derived from our histories. These strategies are most pronounced during moments of vulnerability and our need for connection when our safety or sense of self feels compromised. Action tendencies can be either effective or ineffective. This chapter will help you identify which is true for you. Once clarified, you have the opportunity to explore and create effective strategies for interacting with the people who matter most.

Effective strategies send clear signals to others when we need support. These signals clearly communicate what we feel and what we need, and therefore, allow our recipients to clearly understand us and respond to what we're asking for.

For example, if I am feeling distressed or scared, and I reach out for support, the person for whom I am reaching can easily hear the genuine, personal nature of my request by the *way* I am saying it. The *way* something is said has more resonance than *what* is said and dictates whether our words invite people to come toward us or push them away during our moments of need. The *way* we communicate in these key moments has the effect of engendering their compassion, care, and interest in being there for us, as well as the opposite.

We previously defined addiction as an action tendency that has an adaptive purpose. If our lives have played out in such a way that when the going gets tough we go it alone, we don't reach out to people one way or another. Instead, we found a way to cope with emotional pain: we use.

Addiction was never nature's intended response for coping with painful emotional experiences. At some point in your life, addiction became the understandable choice and behavior, but addiction is far from natural.

There was a time prior to using addictive substances that your primary action tendency during moments of distress and vulnerability was different. However, given the circumstances, our original attachment experiences produced action tendencies that were not sufficient to elicit the essential responsiveness and care that you needed, so you turned to an alternative action tendency: addiction.

Identifying your initial strategies that preexisted addiction will help to clarify your emotional and personal context. This process will generate insight into the strengths and limitations of the strategies that were developed long before addiction was a part of your life. Your early action tendencies had limitations. They were not successfully getting you the support that you were seeking, or addiction would not have even been a consideration.

The following exercises will help you to identify and understand your original action tendencies and support you on your journey to implement new strategies for coping with the very same painful emotions without needing to use. Getting clarity on what our old strategies were trying to accomplish is extraordinarily important. All action tendencies, regardless of their effectiveness, were attempts at communicating something important. This next exercise is intended as a laboratory for you to identify where your action tendencies came from and clarify their intended purpose. Note how these old action tendencies prevented the interactions you were seeking from taking place.

Discovering the Relational Environments
That Shaped Your Action Tendencies

When emotional pain intensified and persisted, using your substance or behavior of choice became the default mechanism for managing distress and isolation. Let's peel the layers of this onion back even further so that we can begin to understand what interfered with being able to effectively reach out to others when you were needing comfort, care, and connection. Place a checkmark next to the two areas that impact you the most:

- ☐ My self-esteem and how I see and feel about myself
- ☐ How I feel seen and perceived by others
- ☐ My ability to attain my personal accomplishments, goals, and aspirations
- ☐ Showing up in a meaningful way in my relationships
- ☐ Staying true to my core values
- ☐ My ability to cope with life's challenges
- ☐ My capacity for joy, happiness, and contentment

Refer to the previous two chapters and revisit what you wrote for the two areas you just selected regarding your inner narratives and feelings that were activated by difficult cues from your life. Write down what is happening inside of you right now as your read through these themes.

_____

_____

_____

_____

_____

_____

_____

In your family of origin, or younger years, whom did you long to turn for reassurance and support when life's seas became choppy? List three to five people:

1. _____

2. _____

3. _____

4. _____

5. _____

What was it about each person you listed that made them important enough to include them here?

_____

_____

_____

_____

_____

What type of responses did you actually receive from these key people whom you longed for connection with?

_____

_____

_____

_____

_____

_____

What was the impact, the personal and emotional effect that their interactions had on you?

_____

_____

_____

_____

_____

_____

How did their responses influence you having to *adapt* your *way* of reaching out to others in moments of challenge and vulnerability?

_____

_____

_____

_____

_____

_____

What type of responses did you receive from your *adaptive* interactions with the key people in your life?

_____

_____

_____

_____

_____

_____

Present moment reflection: How has your *adaptive way* of approaching key people in your life become an obstacle to them being able to be responsive to you when you really need them?

_____

_____

_____

_____

_____

_____

Reflect upon your longing to reach out to the people above, and then having received the types of responses that you just listed. What lessons did you learn from these experiences that influence who you are today?

_____

_____

_____

_____

_____

_____

_____

How is it to reflect upon the *adaptations* you had to make when you couldn't reach out to others from an open, vulnerable state?

_____

_____

_____

_____

_____

_____

Lastly, how has this influenced the way that you currently interact with others in important emotionally charged moments? Place a checkmark next to all that seem fitting.

☐ I avoid people and don't reach out

☐ I blow up, get angry, and demand what I need

☐ I become agitated, clingy, and anxious, often not expressing myself well

☐ I worry a lot

☐ I numb out and shut down

☐ I go it alone

☐ I go into "I hate you; don't leave me" mode

☐ I reach out directly and vulnerably to ask others for what I need

Write down at least one clear example of you engaging with others in one of the ways listed above.

_____

_____

_____

_____

_____

_____

Reflections on your original action tendency:

What is it like to see the workings of your action tendency?

_____

_____

_____

_____

_____

How has this action tendency influenced your attachment wiring as it pertains to reaching out, leaning into, and trusting other people to really be there for you when you need them?

_____

_____

_____

_____

_____

Putting these pieces together, do your best to describe how you understand how these action tendencies came to be in the first place.

_____

_____

_____

_____

_____

Circle back to chapter 4 and locate the graph at the end of the chapter. Notice where you placed yourself within the four quadrants. Now that you know how your circuitry was impacted and rewired through the ups and down of your life and have become knowledgeable about the arc of the internal emotional experiences that prime your addictive behavior, write what it is like to see and understand how you arrived at the attachment strategy you see on the graph.

_____

_____

_____

_____

_____

Exploring Your Attachment Options in Real Time

Select a person who feels safe. You can also choose someone from the list above with whom you've longed to connect in times of need. Either way, choose a person with whom you feel comfortable working on attachment in person.

Anticipate obstacles to reaching out directly. What are you worried about that could go poorly?

_____

_____

_____

_____

_____

_____

_____

Anticipating these obstacles, what are some alternative ways that you could approach this person to help the conversation go well?

_____

_____

_____

_____

_____

_____

_____

_____

Have a preliminary conversation about opening up to them. Let them know that you aren't asking them to fix, solve, or give you advice but rather to simply engage with you with care and interest in both **what** you are saying and the fact that you are **openly reaching out** to them.

How are you feeling as you prepare to take this risk?

_____

_____

_____

_____

_____

_____

_____

_____

After you speak with your chosen person, write about how it worked out. Describe how you are feeling about taking the risk. Describe what the quality of the conversation felt like to you.

_____

_____

_____

_____

_____

_____

_____

_____

_____

Way to go for taking such an enormous risk! That was amazing, and I know that it required a lot of strength and courage to lean in when connection hasn't gone so well in the past. Hopefully, it worked out well. If so, you are actively in the process of creating a new template for how to cope with distress *without* using drugs and alcohol! The next goal will be to make this connection a staple in your life rather than a one-off.

Emotional Process Cheat Sheet

To condense everything that you have identified about the underlying mechanisms of emotion that have been driving your addictive processes, you can refer to the following statement. First, fill in the blanks to complete it.

When I experience (*cue*) _____, I tell myself (*inner narrative*)

_____

_____ about myself. When I tell myself this, I feel (*feelings*)

_____

_____

To help me with these difficult feelings, I want to use. In the moment when I use (*avoidance strategy of action tendency*), I end up feeling _____

_____

_____.

Now, I am discovering new alternate and healthy possibilities. I can reach out to (*approach strategy of action tendency*) _____

_____

_____.

I can do so in this new and more effective way: _____

_____

_____

_____

_____

Congratulations! The four components of emotion that you have been exploring offer crucial information for you to be able to understand the very subtle yet extremely potent forces that often remain unconscious which have been activating your addiction.

The way that you have just condensed your awareness of a very nuanced emotional process is quite extraordinary. I applaud you for your hard work. I know that this journey is not easy, but neither is living with all that dormant pain that has been fueling your addiction for all these years. This cheat sheet gives you an opportunity to taste the fruits of your hard-won labor. Practice this every day, and your ability to become more finely attuned to your inner world and make choices that nourish your well-being will gain momentum week by week. Nothing can replace repetition. Use this cheat sheet often and you will see the results in your life. You will no longer be held hostage to your addictive processes.

CHAPTER 9

Breaking the Bonds of Insecure Attachment

Relationship distress is one of the most predictable triggers for relapse. Relationships also happen to be one of the most significant preventive factors to buffer us from the vicious cycle of addiction. Safe supportive relationships are not simply luck of the draw. They can be created intentionally with people who are available and capable of doing so with us. Thankfully there are known building blocks for creating solid and dependable relationships that are a source of joy, connection, and support. This is the essence of what secure attachment provides for us. There is a path for transforming insecure attachment into a well-integrated secure attachment. It is called *earned secure attachment*. Earned secure attachment can be achieved at any time in your life. It offers a way to relate clearly and effectively within our relationships. Creating securely attached relationships that we can rely on in tough times is the key to breaking the vicious cycle of addiction.

The Stories of Juan and Janine

Juan and Janine came to see me after Janine's last intensive outpatient treatment program. Her recovery had been permeated with slips for the previous nine months. Janine managed her grandparents' grocery store, worked very hard, and helped their business thrive. At home, however, she found herself frequently struggling when her partner, Juan, would spend time with his friends. In their worst moments of conflict, Janine would escalate into anger, derision, name calling, and sometimes rage. This would predictably push Juan away.

The unresolved tensions between them became an ingredient in her slips. As she explored these moments of escalating conflict, she got in touch with how terrified and depressed she felt as a child. Back then, Janine would slip into a dark hole, feel hopeless, and have to navigate the chaotic and violent fighting going on in her home all by herself.

As a child, when things were at their worst, Janine discovered she could generate anger. Her rage would energize her so that she could mobilize through her depression, get herself up and out the door to school, and ultimately get good grades. Anger became her lifeline. However, the strategy that helped her survive her childhood was severely damaging her relationship as an adult. Predictably, the residual pain and distress from her relationship jeopardized her recovery.

This new realization allowed her reach out to Juan directly when she was hurting, feeling insecure, or grabbed by fear. The calm, open, and vulnerable way that she approached him invited him to ride alongside her in these difficult moments rather than feel pushed away by her anger. Discovering the function and intention of *your* strategies will give you the information you need to be able to connect effectively with the significant others and important people in your life when it's most important.

Messages Sent Through Insecure Attachment Strategies

This chapter will help you clarify the role your attachment tendencies have played in your life and learn from the experiences you've had in key moments with important people in your life.

Examine the following chart that identifies common action tendencies associated with each attachment strategy. Notice what happens inside of you as you read the tendencies associated with your strategy to yourself.

Secure Attachment Strategy	Avoidant Strategy	Anxious Strategy	Fearful-Avoidant Strategy
Directly approach key people in my life when I need them	Go it alone and don't rely on others	Criticize, complain, accuse, and find fault	Push people away, yet simultaneously crave closeness
Calmly and clearly share my thoughts	Overly focus on the needs of others	Make demands rather than requests	Blow up and lash out
Reach out to discuss what I'm feeling	Keep my feelings inside	Pursue, push, poke, and badger	Hurt myself, put myself down
Express myself openly	Dismiss the need for relationships	Have difficulty owning my part in conflict	Insist and demand that others be there for me
Reach out to ask for reassurance when I need it	Accommodate, placate, people-please	Frequently blame my partner	Shut down, shut people out, and go away
Lean into the people closest to me for comfort, care, and connection	Numb out	Lash out and get angry, and blame people close to me during conflict	Lose control and become easily overwhelmed by my emotions
Take the risk to discuss difficult topics	Shut down	Escalate emotionally	Desperately seek connection
Share my personal feelings with people with whom I am close	Avoid	Turn my fears and needs into an attack	Panic when I'm alone

Write down what you just noticed getting kicked up inside you from reading the responses most related to your strategy.

_____

_____

_____

_____

_____

Placing *your* strategy under the microscope will help you discover the unintentional *impact* of your reaction (how it has contributed to you not getting what you are seeking) and the meaningful *intention* beneath your strategy (what you are genuinely wanting and hoping to communicate). The next set of exercises is aimed at helping you to discover the truth of your strategy's intention, or purpose. This information will help you refine your strategy so that you can elicit the response that you are longing for and create the connections that you desire.

Discovering the True Intention Beneath Your Action Tendencies

Think back to a recent situation in which you were communicating with a significant other or someone very important to you and it turned into conflict, misunderstanding, disagreements, or fighting. Try to come up with three examples. Below, name the person and briefly describe the situation, your reaction, and their reaction.

Example #1:

The person: _____

The situation: _____

_____

_____

_____

_____

Your reaction: _____

_____

_____

_____

_____

Their reaction: _____

_____

_____

_____

_____

Example #2:

The person: _____

The situation: _____

_____

_____

_____

_____

Your reaction: _____

_____

_____

_____

_____

Their reaction: _____

_____

_____

_____

_____

Example #3:

The person: _____

The situation: _____

_____

_____

_____

_____

Your reaction: _____

_____

_____

_____

_____

_____

Their reaction: _____

_____

_____

_____

_____

Assess your answers for themes and commonalities that you identified within the three situations.

How might your action tendency (insecure attachment strategy) have influenced the other person's reaction?

_____

_____

_____

What potential negative messages does your action tendency send?

_____

_____

_____

What is the message that you actually want others to receive from you?

_____

_____

_____

What kind of response were you truly hoping for?

_____

_____

_____

Breaking Toxic Patterns of Disconnection Within Our Most Important Relationships

The following diagram is designed to clarify the powerful process that transforms our greatest resource for protecting us from addiction—our relationships with significant others—into fertile ground for addictive processes to take hold.

Those who matter most to us are unique in that they are the people from whom we need support, protection, love, and a sense of belonging. Being on the receiving end of their insecure attachment reactions (yelling, name calling, escalations, blaming, stone walling, neglect, abuse) not only hurts, but naturally creates intense personal meaning (for example, *they must hate me, they think I am ridiculous, they so easily prioritize everybody and everything other than me, they couldn't care less about me*...or perhaps, even worse, *they are dangerous, vicious, and out to harm me*).

These painful narratives eventually take root deep within us and become unleased during moments of conflict. Emotionally, they hurt like hell. When our narratives generate enough emotional distress, they propel us into a reaction. We fight back, we shut down, or use again as a result. We're left feeling hopeless and overwhelmed.

In the diagram below, arrows point directly through the "infinity loop" demonstrating how each partner's insecure attachment strategies activate these internal personal narratives and emotional raw spots. Once the narratives gain momentum, and intensify our emotional pain, we respond by reacting to our partner through our own insecure strategies.

In conflict with the most important people in our lives, only the surface-experience: trigger/reaction is visible. There is rarely any indication of the deeper meaning of what these moments mean to us or the emotional distress we are contending with. The absence of sharing what is experienced beneath the surface only reinforces the negative narratives and assumptions that we (as well as the other) hold when this dynamic occurs. A self-reinforcing, vicious cycle is created and causes further alienation between us and our loved ones.

THE NEGATIVE RELATIONSHIP CYCLE

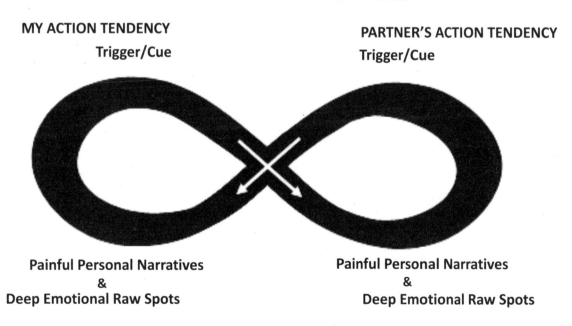

Adapted from Dr. Scott Woolley

Mapping Your Steps in the Dance of Disconnection

Choose one example of a recent situation from the previous exercise that best exemplifies a moment of vulnerability or need to really be seen, heard, or understood. Respond to the prompts, giving particular attention to how the person reacted.

Their action tendency (attachment strategy) that became my cue was: _____

_____

What did they say? What did they do?

_____

_____

_____

_____

What were their nonverbal expressions: tones of voice, facial expressions, body language?

_____

_____

_____

_____

My negative inner narratives

What did their action tendency (attachment strategy) mean to you? What was the implied message? In what ways does it feel familiar?

_____

_____

_____

_____

Describe what this implies about how they see or feel about you in these moments.

_____

_____

_____

_____

How does this impact your sense of feeling cared about and understood?

_____

_____

_____

_____

My inner feelings

In moments like this, list the feelings that get stirred up inside of you when all of the above are activated.

_____

_____

_____

_____

The messages I'm sending

What kind of impression do you give off in these moments of need?

_____

_____

_____

_____

What is it like when these impressions eclipse the real intentions and needs that you wish to express in these moments?

_____

_____

_____

_____

My action tendency (attachment strategy) when I am distressed

How do I respond to conflict with loved ones? What is it that I do, say, or feel inclined to do in these really hard situations?

_____

_____

_____

_____

_____

Completing the cycle

When I react this way, my action tendency is: _____

My loved one responds and reacts by: _____

Describe how this impacts your relationship with this person in terms of emotional safety, comfort, and connection:

_____

_____

_____

_____

_____

Addiction and my relationship strategies: Tying this all together

What is the likelihood of you being able to lean into this person for support and reassurance when the going gets tough? What is the likelihood of you turning to your substance or behavior of choice?

_____

_____

_____

Can your loved one see, understand, or receive your intentions?

_____

_____

_____

What is the impact on you when your intentions become eclipsed by your action tendency?

_____

_____

_____

How do these negative patterns further set you up for the possibility of using during stressful times and life challenges?

_____

_____

_____

These negative patterns create communication firewalls that prevent empathy, understanding, and care in our most important relationships. They transform our best sources of reliable support into demoralizing experiences of loneliness, misunderstanding, and conflict. In time, these patterns solidify and become rigid default dynamics between us and the people who care about us the most. They hijack our relationships and leave us isolated and alone...again. The likelihood of turning to our drugs of choice for some semblance of relief skyrockets. Our substances and addictive behaviors become the replacement for secure attachment.

Your explorations in this chapter have given you precise data for discovering and identifying what would be most useful to communicate during these significant interactions. We will use this information to curate your own personal way of effectively expressing yourself to receive exactly what you have been wanting and needing from the people you love in these challenging moments. The information you discovered is the first step toward creating relationships that heal within your own life. This will begin to pave the path for your most important relationships to become the substitute replacement for addiction.

You may also consider sharing this work with the important people in your life. They also unintentionally get in their own way of expressing themselves clearly and directly to you. Explain how the cycle creates a dance of disconnection and share the discoveries that you have made. Invite them to explore their side of the street. Once they have done so, the two of you can compare notes and map out both sides of the cycle, so that you can see the dance in its entirety. Sharing with an important person, should you attempt it, will serve as a springboard into what we will be exploring in the next chapter: How to actually create relationships that heal.

CHAPTER 10

Creating Relationships That Heal

Creating securely attached relationships is the royal road to transforming our relationship to addiction. It is perhaps the most important factor for inoculating us against addiction. Given that the primary function of addictive processes is to self-medicate emotional distress through the solitary act of using, secure attachment utilizes nature's hardwired method of regulating overwhelming emotion: reaching out, leaning in, and connecting with people who love and care about us.

Both secure and insecure attachment are created and maintained through the habitual way that we communicate with others. It is crucial that our attachment strategies are in sync with our genuine intentions. Otherwise, we can unintentionally send very confusing, or alienating messages to our loved ones, and then wonder why they either respond to us harshly or ignore us in moments when we really need a caring response. Over time these interactions become corrosive to the relationships that we cherish the most. Our patterns of attachment can either demoralize us and the people we are in relationship with or create strong and lasting connections. The following story is a wonderful example of both sides of this equation.

The Stories of Marlyne and Mikey

Marlyne and Mikey created a thriving relationship for more than a decade. They successfully achieved major milestones in life: finding meaningful work in the same city after graduate school, getting quickly promoted, beginning a lovely family with two healthy children, and settling into a nice groove in their lives.

Marlyne quickly gained visibility and prestige at her job. Her income rose significantly as a result, as did her status within her field. However, during a corporate reorganization she went from being a rising star with a bright future to a falling star without no path in sight. Despite her significant contributions to the company, she was given a moderate severance package and little recognition or appreciation for all her hard work.

Meanwhile, Mikey continued to advance in his career slowly and surely. He was given a broader territory and a larger group of coworkers to report directly to him. However, his time was no longer his own. Significant tension developed between Mikey and Marlyne. Conflict and sniping at each other became commonplace, and they found themselves frequently irritated with one another.

Marlyne's drinking escalated after years of well-managed moderation. Episodes of intoxicated belligerence permeated their lives. Marlyne would escalate, sling sharp accusations at Mikey, and rarely apologize. As a result, Mikey conveniently threw himself further into work, staying late at the office to avoid Marlyne.

They came to see me to improve their relationship. Thankfully their relationship had good bones despite the current tensions. Still, the recent hostility was corrosive to their deep bond and the gap between them progressively widened.

As we began exploring Marlyne's emotional escalations, she dissolved into tears. She said, "As you were climbing the corporate ladder, I was in free fall. I felt like I didn't matter to you anymore. I couldn't get your attention. You didn't understand the depth of my pain and loss. You seemed to not even care. The only way that I can get your attention is by getting loud, and I'll admit it, even mean at times. I need you, of all people, to really get what I am going through. You are totally consumed with your world. I feel like my world is completely invisible to you."

When Marlyne spoke from a place of such authentic vulnerability rather than attacking and reacting, she conveyed the true *intentions* that she had been desperately longing for Mikey to understand. Marlyne was beginning to see how the impact of her reactive escalations was creating the very thing she feared the most: Mikey pulling away from her. This further intensified her pain. She found herself self-medicating the pain with alcohol.

Marlyne discovered that the force behind her reactivity and anger had been her desire to feel understood by Mikey. She longed for him to be by her side during this awful time of loss and confusion. This revelation opened the door to finding clear and direct ways to share her thoughts, feelings, and needs with him.

She discovered that it felt safer to lash out and send a sideways signal than to express herself vulnerably with him. After wrestling with her fear, she took a risk and opened up about her hurt and loneliness with him from a softer place.

As she learned to reach out to Mikey in ways that he could clearly understand, he was able to better support her, and her drinking subsided. She was finally communicating in a way that expressed her personal *intentions*—being seen and cared for—that she longed for him to understand. Mikey was no longer responding to the emotional weapon of her anger and instead felt compassionately drawn to Marlyne in her moments of hurt and sadness. His presence and support meant that she no longer had to cope alone. The relationship became solid ground for them once again, and her drinking was replaced with the reliable connection that the two of them were able to create.

Interestingly, it is through relationship that we find our sense of individuation, independence, sense of self, and trust in others. It was working through difficulty that pushed Mikey and Marlyne to lean in, open up, and share their scariest vulnerabilities with one another.

This example illuminates what secure attachment offers us. We find our true, strong, individual selves not simply through the skills and techniques of self-soothing but also from the integrity and courage required to be open and vulnerable. This openness mirrors how our sense of self was when we were young, before we began encountering the distress of our early lives. And as John Bowlby, the psychoanalyst who created attachment theory, said, attachment runs "from the cradle to the grave."

Through EFT, Mikey and Marlyne were able to harness the power of attachment to thrive and become their best, wisest, strongest selves. With their newfound abilities to understand themselves, express themselves clearly, risk with one another, and assert themselves, their relationship continued to support them to be the best of who they were. Their individuality infused the relationship with strength and love, and the relationship, in turn, supported them to be their best selves. There was no need or place for addictive processes to take hold. Not only was Marlyne able to process and let go of her fear, but she also soon became the director of an innovative company!

After reading Mikey and Marlyne's story, take a moment for reflection. What does it stir within you? What hopes, possibilities, and opportunities come to mind after reading their story?

_____

_____

_____

_____

_____

_____

_____

_____

_____

_____

A.R.E.: The Building Blocks of Securely Attached Relationships

Dr. Susan Johnson, the originator of EFT, created the acronym A.R.E. to identify qualities of interaction that foster emotional connection and secure attachment in relationships: accessibility, responsiveness, and emotional engagement. When *impact* is aligned with our genuine emotional *intentions*, the qualities of A.R.E. are inherently present. When the elements of A.R.E. are consistently active in a relationship, they build an incredibly secure foundation between people. Over time, A.R.E. create and maintain secure attachment. Conversely, the lack of A.R.E. can result in insecure attachment and distress between loved ones.

- **Accessibility:** Can you reach your partner? Living life to its fullest requires being able to share the highs and the lows with people who really matter. When you are struggling, feeling overwhelmed and down on yourself, knowing that your partner is available and can be reached is crucial. When your partner is accessible, you can travel the journey of life together. However, when you are not able to reliably access your partner, it makes your pain exponentially worse.

- **Responsiveness:** When we share something important, and we receive a response that tells us that our partner really cares about what we're talking about, there is both a sense of connection and a deep feeling that we are meaningful to them. We feel a clear sense of resonance. We feel felt. Conversely, when people respond using the "right" words, but we know that they aren't actually paying attention or worse, they don't really give a damn, it is demoralizing and disconnecting. Being ignored, stonewalled, and getting no response in the dance of attachment signals that we are irrelevant to the people who matter most.

- **Emotional engagement:** When we lean into the people who mean the most to us and we feel their care—they are present and respond in a way that is really dialed in to what we are feeling and saying—the quality of connection is beyond words. We know it in our bones. This is emotional engagement. It's the icing on the cake of accessibility and responsiveness.

Creating A.R.E. Interactions

Now, let's dig in a little deeper to understand the difference between *attuned* interactions (supportive, connective, A.R.E. interactions) and *misattuned* interactions (distancing, out of sync, absent of A.R.E.). The following exercise uses examples from a romantic partnership. However, the building blocks for secure relationships are the same for any deeply important relationship in your life.

As you do this next exercise, pay attention to what comes alive inside of you when you read the attuned responses. In contrast, notice what comes alive inside of you when you read and experience the misattuned responses. Then, write a few sentences about each.

Which of the following are examples of *accessibility*? Circle your answers.

A) Your partner is ready and available to finish the difficult conversation at the time the two of you agreed upon.

B) As you get to the most difficult part of the conversation and begin getting choked up, your partner picks up their phone to check their messages.

C) As your partner shares their fears with you for the very first time, you reach out and gently put a hand on their shoulder.

D) When you finally get home from a terrible day at work hoping for a conversation and perhaps a hug, you find your partner out with their friends...once again.

E) You try to get your partner's attention to share with them that you were accepted to the college of your choice, and they snap at you to be quiet until they're finished watching TV.

Reflection on the attuned responses:

_____

_____

_____

_____

_____

_____

Reflection on the misattuned responses:

_____

_____

_____

_____

_____

_____

Which of the following are examples of *responsiveness*? Circle your answers.

A) Person #1: My closest cousin was in a car accident today.

Person #2: That sounds awful; are you okay? I'm here to talk if you would like.

B) Person #1: My closest cousin was in a car accident today.

Person #2: My buddy's cousin is also a horrible driver.

C) Person #1: My closest cousin was in a car accident today.

Person #2: Did you ever get my book back from him?

D) Person #1: My closest cousin was in a car accident today.

Person #2: Oh my God, he was like a brother to you. That sounds overwhelming.

E) Person #1: My closest cousin was in a car accident today.

Person #2: (not even looking up from the computer) Bummer. Life is rough.

Reflection on the attuned responses:

_____

_____

_____

_____

_____

Reflection on the misattuned responses:

_____

_____

_____

_____

_____

Which of the following are examples of *emotional* engagement? Circle your answers.

A) (in a loud, quick, and impatient tone) You know I love you. Why do you have to ask me over and over again?

B) You are never here for me; you couldn't care less how bad it hurts. I am always the last one to get any kind of consideration. You are just like the rest of them.

C) That argument that we had yesterday really shook me up. I know I wasn't in the best place to have a conversation. I would really love to see if we can find a way to talk this through together.

D) I know that you were really struggling yesterday when you shouted at me. I'm guessing you just had a really bad day. I'm game to talk if you want to.

E) Who are you to tell me to calm down? You are the one always picking fights.

Reflection on the attuned responses:

_____

_____

_____

_____

_____

_____

Reflection on the misattuned responses:

_____

_____

_____

_____

_____

_____

Answer key: For accessibility, if you circled A and C, you are correct! For responsiveness, if you circled A and D, you are correct! For emotional engagement, if you circled C and D, you are correct!

What was it like to *feel* the contrast inside of yourself between attuned (connecting) responses, and the misattuned (disconnecting) responses?

_____

_____

_____

_____

_____

_____

_____

Using A.R.E. in times of crisis and need is the most important communication tool available to us. These tools become crucial when our world gets rocked and we are struggling. This has a lot to do with addiction. Instead of using, we can draw on strong, caring, and supportive people to help us navigate life's ups and downs.

Expressing Intentions Clearly

Think of two recent examples in which you used an ineffective attachment strategy (escalating, criticizing, demanding, getting angry, or the opposite: shutting down, numbing out, avoiding). Give some thought to examining what you were *intending* to express through the way you reacted, not simply the words you said.

Example #1: _____

_____

What was I *intending* to communicate through the way I was reacting in that moment?

_____

_____

_____

_____

_____

What was the response that I had hoped to receive?

_____

_____

_____

_____

How could I alter my communication, so I more effectively convey my intentions?

_____

_____

_____

_____

Example #2: _____

_____

What was I *intending* to communicate through the way I was reacting in that moment?

_____

_____

_____

_____

_____

What was the response that I had hoped to receive?

_____

_____

_____

_____

How could I alter my communication, so I more effectively convey my intentions?

_____

_____

_____

_____

Tools for Creating Relationships That Heal

The following exercises are designed to expand your emotional range and abilities—your *emotional intelligence*.

These exercises offer you ways to communicate more effectively with the people who really matter in your life. They are designed to help you become more able to express your inner world and more able to be receptive to theirs. These exercises will also help you send clear signals, so people can be responsive to you, especially when you really need them.

Begin with the Partner Appreciation exercise. It sets a lovely tone for care, safety, and mutual respect. When you are ready, move on to the Feeling Word exercise; it is designed to increase your emotional vocabulary, expand your range of expression, and help you better tolerate feeling emotions.

The last two exercises are more advanced. Approach them thoughtfully; try each one once per week for the next two weeks. Record your results below. Good luck! And enjoy!

Partner Appreciation

This activity requires two people, so grab your important person. Find a comfortable space where you can face each other.

1. Take turns sharing specific things you appreciate about each other.

2. Take the time to explain why.

That is all! This exercise helps you and the important people in your life build positive emotional connections for a stronger recovery. It promotes acknowledgment of the positive and meaningful sentiments that often are left unspoken. You are depositing social capital in the heart-bank. In turn, people will be more receptive and available to you, and when you have a dustup (or make a withdrawal), it won't empty the account like your addiction used to do.

Feeling Word

This activity also requires two people, so grab your important person. Find a comfortable space where you can face each other.

1. Search for personal feelings and emotions that have been hard to cope with throughout your addictive process.

2. Choose an emotion.

3. Then share stories or experiences (emotional or situational) related to the chosen feeling.

4. Switch roles, so that the other person can share similarly with you.

5. You will be able to create both a path through difficult discussions as well as deepen your abilities to have your partner/person really hear your genuine *intentions*.

This exercise is designed to increase your emotional fluency and range of expression so that you can more readily communicate your intention.

Emotional Reactivity

This exercise helps you and a partner create a path for successfully holding difficult discussions with one another, and greatly increase the likelihood of your intentions being heard.

1. Choose a topic that often leads to escalation or conflict.

2. Practice taking a break when emotions begin to escalate or get intense.

3. Agree to come back later once both of you are calm (fifteen to twenty minutes should do the trick).

4. During the separation time, explore finding a more productive, calm, and connecting style of holding the conversation. Consider: What role did you play in activating your partner's distress? What was the more difficult, deeper meaning of their response to you? How could you approach the conversation differently?

5. Afterward, notice what you did differently and record your responses.

Noticing Avoidance

This exercise may be a little more challenging. It is designed to help you identify the emotional raw spots that get activated during sensitive conversations. Choose a topic that often leads to shutting down, numbing out, or avoiding conflict.

Notice your "departure point"—the point during the conversation when you want to exit or shut down.

Rewind. Take a moment to track your conversation up to the point when emotional raw spots became activated, and you wanted to leave.

Identify the difficult emotions.

Then answer: What would you most want the other person to really understand about your experience?

While remaining with your person, identify how they could assist you in sharing more. Tell them what you need.

Then share at least some of what you most want understood in this moment. Give yourself permission to share as much or little as you are comfortable with. See if you can extend your range over time.

_____

_____

_____

_____

_____

_____

_____

Well done! It is never easy to see, acknowledge, and own our part in how things go south in our relationships. There is also nothing more empowering.

CHAPTER 11

Trauma and Addiction

Unresolved trauma may be the hidden force behind your addiction. Where there is addiction, there is often trauma lurking under the hood. Let's uncover it.

Chapter 5 introduced the promise of natural recovery. An extraordinary amount of research and articles have been written about how consistently people who struggle with addictions to substances quit without any formal type of intervention. The most famous study (National Institutes of Health 2006) with more than 43,000 subjects, found that approximately 75 percent of people did so! For us, this is amazing news.

If 75 percent of people struggling with addiction can quit on their own, who are the 25 percent of people who can't? What makes them different? The adverse childhood experiences (ACEs) study sheds light on this subject.

The ACEs study focused on people struggling with compulsive overeating, a process addiction. They were carefully taught well-researched skills and procedures for healthy eating, which were applied over a significant period of time. Much to the research team's surprise, an enormous number of subjects abandoned everything that they had learned and reverted to their previous unhealthy eating patterns. What happened?

The researchers discovered that participants abandoned their effective protocols not because of a lack of personal willpower or flaws in the treatment design, but rather because of striking similarities in their personal histories: they had suffered multiple traumas and abuses early in their lives.

The research team had inadvertently removed the very thing that the subjects had been using to self-medicate painful emotional distress from their childhoods. Compulsive overeating happened to be the coping strategy that kept the overwhelming pain from the awful events at bay. Without the familiar coping mechanism, the pain surfaced and was so distressing that subjects reverted to unhealthy eating patterns in order to shut it all down. Compulsive overeating was actually an attempted solution to a very secretive and shame-filled problem: multiple traumatic experiences, often occurring during the subject's childhoods. Their addiction was an emotional survival strategy.

Skills and tools for curbing addictive processes are necessary, but for many people, and in many circumstances, they are not sufficient. They are simply not powerful enough to stave off the flood of emotion where trauma is concerned. When those dormant raw spots from the past are activated, most skills can't keep the dam from breaking. We get flooded with pain. This leaves us caught in a bind: using is not the answer, but not using leaves us emotionally overwhelmed and on our own.

Identifying the impact of what you've been through in your life can be a powerful tool in beginning to forgive yourself and understand why changing your relationship to addiction has been so challenging. Studies on ACEs offer insight into how our past trauma affects our current lives. About 64 percent of people have at least one ACE, which can dramatically increase the likelihood of their using drugs or alcohol (Felitti 2002; Swedo et al. 2023).

Identifying Adverse Childhood Experiences

Review the list of adverse childhood experiences. Place a checkmark next to any ACE that took place in your life. If there happens to be a particular category in which you endured multiple experiences of that ACE, write the number on the line. When you complete this list, locate your ACEs score on the circular chart below.

- ☐ Sexual abuse   _____
- ☐ Physical abuse and violence   _____
- ☐ Emotional abuse   _____
- ☐ Physical neglect   _____
- ☐ Emotional neglect   _____
- ☐ Contemptuous separation or divorce   _____
- ☐ Mental illness or suicide within your home   _____
- ☐ Addiction in your home   _____
- ☐ Witnessing violence to a family member   _____
- ☐ A family member incarcerated in prison   _____
- ☐ Poverty: not able to afford basic needs (food, shelter, clothing, medical treatment, and so forth)   _____
- ☐ Witnessing violence in the neighborhood or at school   _____
- ☐ Discrimination (racial, ethnic, religious, sexual, gender, and so forth)   _____

Total ACEs: _____

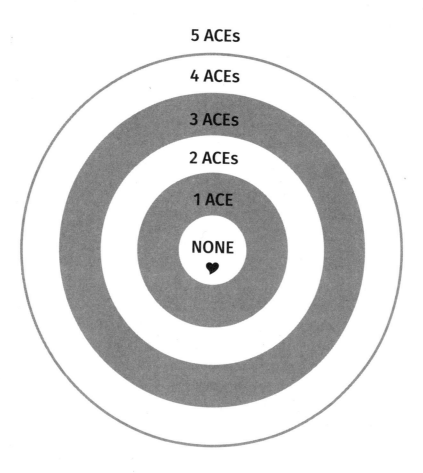

What is it like to review your history and observe your ACEs scores?

_____

_____

_____

_____

_____

How are you doing? That exercise can be very challenging. This is tough stuff. Evaluate your emotional temperature (see chapter 3) and where you are on the experiencing scale. If you are feeling stirred up, find a quiet spot to practice the Three-Part Breath exercise (also in chapter 3) for five minutes. Then return to this book.

Trauma Rewires Our Emotional Circuitry

Through secure attachment we develop the ability to effectively manage our emotional worlds, and gain a sense of happiness, self-confidence, and the ability to create and maintain meaningful relationships. Additionally, being able to effectively regulate affect prevents our system from getting emotionally overloaded and causing us to either shut down or blow up when we are faced with difficult situations. Being able to manage difficulty with integrity and poise provides us with the baseline ability to trust and believe in ourselves and others.

Trauma changes everything. It turns the equation upside down. Consistent early experiences of negativity, fear, and harm create toxic emotional currents that overwhelm our system and require us to adapt our natural wiring. Our natural instinct to lean in, reach out, and seek reassurance from others often becomes extinguished. We are forced to find alternate ways of creating safety.

When trauma occurs during childhood, before we are capable of protecting ourselves and processing these terrible events, unprocessed emotional pain becomes stored in compartments deep within us. Once again, the unconscious process of *compartmentalization* protects us from having to directly face overwhelming distress and potentially become psychologically incapacitated. In the absence of reliable caregivers to lean into for comfort, our unconscious had to step in as if it were a surrogate parent. It removed the pain, the meaning, and even sometimes the memory of awful events to protect our psyche and our emotional self.

Traumatic experiences rewire our neurobiology (van der Kolk 2015). It reroutes our neural circuitry so that it is primed to seek protection rather than connection. When trauma is driving our response to difficult interactions, we often find ourselves blowing up at the people in our lives, shutting them out, or reacting in regretful ways. In dire moments, when the need to trust and rely on others is at its peak, the ghosts of our past experiences are unleashed. The closeness we need becomes terrifying because closeness in the past didn't work out so well. However, experiencing immense distress and being on our own with it is equally intolerable, so we end up seeking relief through our addiction.

Biography and Biology

Suppressing and locking away the pain of past trauma is a predictable survival strategy. It resourced us by preventing us from becoming emotionally or psychologically incapacitated. It may have saved our lives. However, compartmentalization has an enormously important drawback. Its location, however remote, remains *inside* of us and required the ongoing maintenance of addiction to keep it at bay.

This strategy also had a profound impact: it reinforces our inability to trust ourselves and others, the tendency to isolate, and the necessity for continuing to use our substances of choice to keep the lid on the box of all the unprocessed pain and shame.

In order to transcend this self-reinforcing pattern, we must face the fear and pain we compartmentalized so long ago. Otherwise, it will continue to live inside of us. This is easier said than done. As children, we were no match for the reservoir of fear and pain. It would have crushed us. We began compartmentalizing pain so long ago that most of us don't even recognize its existence anymore. The presence, meanings, and emotions associated with these past events faded. However, as long as traumatic material remains dormant and unexamined within us, it will continue to debilitate our lives and happiness (Greenspan 2004). It will continue to invite addiction (Maté 2007).

Thankfully we do not have to dig up and encounter all the traumas of our past to successfully transform our relationship with addiction and heal. However, we do have to find a way in, walk through the door, and venture inside. We must face the pain from our pasts to heal. The only way out is through.

Interpersonal Conflict and Past Trauma

Have you ever wondered why our partners, children, parents, and even the occasional best friend get under our skin in a way that no one else in the world seems to be able to do? Have you ever found yourself saying, "No one in my life seems to negatively impact me the way that they do?"

These important people unwittingly hold the invisible key that fits perfectly into the lock of our inner hidden doorways. Those few people who we let into the inner sanctum of our hearts have access to our unresolved fears, residual emotional pain, and unmet relational longings from the deficits in our attachment histories. They also hold the key to healing our past trauma.

Ironically, it is through the conflicts we have with these core people that we are provided incredible opportunities for untangling the grip of past trauma from our lives (Johnson 2005). Memories of past events may be foggy or nonexistent, but the emotional residue of those awful moments contains hugely important information. The residue becomes visible during present-day interactions, especially during moments of conflict, need, or difficulty. Paying attention to what occurs within us during these highly charged moments can free us from the compartmentalized pain that has been driving our addictive processes.

Using Interpersonal Conflict to Uncover Hidden Doorways to the Past

Let's explore how our most potent resources to buffer us from addiction can also be the most powerful triggers that send us spiraling downward. Review the list of internalized personal and existential messages that we carry from our past trauma. These are the residues of our traumas. Then respond to the writing prompts.

Fears

- Fear of never being successful
- Fear of not finding happiness.
- Fear of always being inadequate
- Fear of failing
- Fear of succeeding
- Fear of being unlovable
- Fear of judgment
- Fear of criticism
- Fear of rejection
- Fear of harm
- Fear of abandonment
- Fear of being alone
- Fear of the unknown
- Fear of being forgotten
- Fear of being lost
- Fear of not being good enough
- Fear of never being liked

Thoughts

- I'm dumb
- I'm ugly
- I'll always mess up
- I'm a burden
- I'm the problem
- I don't deserve love
- I don't deserve forgiveness
- I don't deserve happiness
- I will always be alone
- I will lose the people I love

Consider two conflicts, differences, or negatively charged interactions you recently had with an important person in your life. Consider the messages in the previous list as you respond.

Incident #1

1. What happened?

_____

_____

_____

_____

2. What got to you about it?

_____

_____

_____

_____

3. Write down fears from the list above relevant to this situation.

_____

_____

_____

_____

_____

4. Write down which thoughts accompanied this situation.

_____

_____

_____

_____

5. What were the implied messages it sent you about others in your life?

_____

_____

_____

_____

_____

Incident #2

1. What happened?

_____

_____

_____

_____

2. What got to you about it?

_____

_____

_____

_____

3. Write down fears from the list above relevant to this situation.

_____

_____

_____

_____

_____

4. Write down which thoughts accompanied this situation.

_____

_____

_____

_____

_____

5. What were the implied messages it sent you about others in your life?

_____

_____

_____

_____

_____

This is difficult material. The thoughts and fears that accompany situations like these are deep and painful. Take a moment to reflect on the themes you discovered about the core personal and existential messages you privately carry inside of yourself from the examples above.

_____

_____

_____

_____

_____

_____

_____

_____

_____

If you haven't already, put the book down for a few minutes and practice 5 to 10 rounds of Three-Part Breath (see chapter 3) to recenter yourself. The work you're doing right now is extremely admirable. You are courageously walking the path of the hero's journey. The strength, wisdom, and capability that you are demonstrating is extremely commendable.

Without needing to directly address every traumatic event in your life, understanding the emotional residue that you have been carrying inside offers a pathway to healing. Healing is an inside job. Therefore, healing the emotional impact of these painful messages will allow you to take giant strides in dismantling your addictive processes and heal past traumas. Your behavior and addictive processes are reflective of your inner experience of unprocessed pain from the past. As you continue to process, metabolize, and let go of this pain, you also free yourself from the need to rely upon addictive processes.

Attachment: The True Antidote for Our Painful Past

Let's create some powerful attachment scaffolding to accompany you on your healing journey.

Identify the caring, respectful, supportive, and safe people in your life. If you don't have anyone currently in your life like this, identify meaningful qualities of what you imagine secure attachment figures to possess.

What qualities did you identify?

_____

_____

_____

_____

Find a quiet relaxing place to either sit or lie down and spend a few minutes closing your eyes and getting centered. Once you have settled in, imagine yourself receiving the qualities that you identified.

When you have finished imagining, write down what you noticed.

_____

_____

_____

_____

Record the thoughts that are going through your mind.

_____

_____

_____

_____

Where do you feel this in your body? Include any accompanying physical sensations.

_____

_____

_____

_____

Write down what you are experiencing emotionally as you take this in. Take your time to savor this experience and allow it to anchor itself within you.

_____

_____

_____

_____

While continuing to experience qualities of secure attachment, notice what happens inside of you as you allow yourself to encounter any negative thoughts that come up.

_____

_____

_____

_____

Imagine what it would have been like to have had these attachment figures available and responsive to you when these tough things happened.

_____

_____

_____

_____

_____

How would this have influenced your life?

_____

_____

_____

_____

What new possibilities might that have opened up for you?

_____

_____

_____

_____

Continue to experience this positive space in the present moment and write down ways that you could bring this into your life today.

_____

_____

_____

_____

Practice this last exercise throughout this upcoming week. Please be patient with yourself. You are performing long-overdue emotional house cleaning. The cleaner your house becomes, the more you will feel better about yourself, others, and the possibilities for your life. In doing so, you will effectively disempower the drivers of your addiction and transform your relationship with addictive processes.

CHAPTER 12

Healing Shame

As you began exploring the residual scars left behind by past traumas, you may have felt the urge to recoil. Facing trauma means facing shame. Facing shame requires great courage. This often feels like making a deliberate decision to run directly into a burning building. The closer you get to it, the more you feel the waves of infernal heat. Initially, this can feel intolerable.

If you find yourself thinking, "I will be incinerated if I go any further. Maybe it would be better to batten the hatches and close back up my inner world," you are not alone. This is hard stuff. However, by now you understand that closing yourself off is destined to backfire. What is it that becomes so overwhelming about this terrain? This first "heat wave" is fear. Before going any further, let's get curious about this. What is so scary about opening the door to your own burning building?

Write a paragraph to yourself about any fears you have about what you may encounter as you take the next steps along your journey of healing.

_____

_____

_____

_____

_____

_____

_____

_____

_____

There is fear, of course. That makes perfect sense. But the real culprit is...shame. Shame and trauma go hand in hand. Shame makes it very difficult to separate the traumatic and painful events that we endured earlier in life from the dark narratives we secretly tell ourselves about who and what we are. The worst part is that we believe the stories.

This is shame. It is the most overwhelming emotional experience that we can encounter because it attacks the very essence of who we are.

Here is the secret that shame does not want you to know: shame must stay hidden to remain intact. It prompts us to hide and avoid the things we feel ashamed about. Secrecy keeps shame alive. Given enough time without intervention, we begin to believe that these narratives are true. They ultimately become our identity. This is precisely what makes shame such a powerful force.

Shame is about *who* not *what*. It becomes the enemy within. Wherever we go, there we are. Chronic shame creates the most vicious cycle of all: it keeps us eternally hiding from ourselves. We can't escape ourselves. When you scratch the surface of addiction, beneath it you find trauma. What happens when you scratch the surface of trauma? You run headlong into intolerable shame.

Why Shame?

Where does shame come from? Shame is quite complex; however, the seeds of shame are often planted in the past from countless negative interactions and events that were never accompanied with repair.

It is one thing to be hurt or harmed and have the person who committed the harm express remorse. This conveys the message that we mean enough to the person who hurt us that they wanted to make sure that we were okay. Responses like these let us know that we are important to them and that being in relationship with us is also meaningful to them. Pain, ill will, and negative feelings resolve naturally, and we move on without painful emotional residue accumulating.

It is another thing to be hurt or harmed and have the person who committed the harm express no remorse. Harming interactions range from criticisms and judgments to violence, abuse, and neglect—absent of any caring response. All that remains is the emotional residue. We are left with a horrifically negative view of ourselves and others. We carry these into our lives. This is shame.

The closer the people who have harmed us are to the inner sanctum of our hearts, the deeper the wound. They have the most direct access to the deepest parts of us. We trust those close to us to protect, support, and care for us. They are the people to whom we want to matter. Therefore, when partners, spouses, best friends, or family members hurt us and don't repair, the pain is exponentially more harmful to our identity.

Shame is also created from broader oppressive systems that abuse power and privilege. Those of us who carry nondominant identities with regard to race, ethnicity, religious affiliation, sexual orientation, or gender identification know a thing or three about this from the ongoing othering and intrinsic microaggressions that occur in everyday life. These messages and actions are deeply woven into our communities. They relegate us to lower levels of status or importance based on characteristics and differences which distinguish us from the dominant majority. These repetitive messages and experiences become internalized as well. We live with the ongoing sense of being personally "less than" from simply being in the world. In essence, shame carries within us the disappointment and dislike of others—as if it were our own.

Tolerating the Fire of Emotion

It is important to acknowledge that, as you courageously explore your inner world, it is predictable to feel emotionally flooded. That is not the intention of this work. However, it's a genuine possibility that merits mentioning. As you have been working your way through this book you may have noticed that your ability to tolerate emotional experience has been growing. If so, huge congratulations to you! However, shame and its accompanying awful inner narratives can overwhelm the best of us.

Before going any further, it is important to locate where you are on the continuum of tolerating emotional experience (see chapter 3). A side effect of addiction is that it effectively turns down the dimmer switch of emotional awareness as a protective barrier from the overwhelm of facing our pain alone. The earlier in life we had to turn it down, the less emotionally fluent we became. The less experience we've had with our emotional worlds, the more intolerable the heat will be when we approach the burning buildings of our past.

Chronic addictive processes prevent us from facing life on life's terms. They block us from directly facing the challenges that come our way and from learning how to successfully navigate them. Although it may appear easier to avoid feeling overwhelmed or frightened, avoidance robs us of two crucial abilities: learning how to persevere in the face of life's challenges and experiencing success.

Avoidance keeps us stuck within false, life-depleting narratives. The more we avoid, the more it gives credence to our fears. Our fears reinforce old, uncontested narratives. These narratives give off more fear. More fear means we are more likely to use. This cycle prevents growth. We miss out on engaging with challenges that offer us opportunities to find solutions and, ultimately, the ability to trust ourselves.

The Window of Tolerance

The *window of tolerance* is a gauge to help you to better understand your ability to remain present, open, and responsive when you encounter challenging emotions and life experiences. This information is designed to help you develop the ability to remain in the middle "window" as often as possible for optimal functioning and emotional balance. Shame and fear are the two most destabilizing emotions: They hold the potential to knock us out of our window of tolerance. When we fall outside of our window of tolerance, we shut down or get flooded with emotion and cannot process or navigate the situations we face.

WINDOW OF TOLERANCE

Hyperarousal/ Hyperactivating		Emotional Equilibrium/ Optimal Functioning		Hypoarousal/ Deactivating
High Risk of Using		**Reaching Out Leaning In**		**High Risk of Using**
• Raging		• Relaxed		• Isolating
• Attacking		• Emotionally clear		• Disconnecting
• Defending		• Emotionally balanced		• Shutting down
• Blaming		• Calm state		• Detaching
• Extensive Worrying		• Able to process effectively		• Avoiding
• Panicking		• Receptive		• Dissociating
• Escalating				• Distancing
• Ruminating				• Numbing

Expanding your window of tolerance strengthens your ability to engage with emotion, accurately process what is occurring, and respond effectively in the moment. Tipping into *hyperarousal*, emotionally floods our limbic system rendering us unable to clearly analyze and process what is happening. It overwhelms our circuitry, depriving us of meaning from the challenges we encounter.

Conversely, when we tip into *hypoarousal*, our cortex overrides our emotions, and at best we go into our heads, or worse we dissociate and don't allow ourselves to feel. *Hypoarousal* insulates us from events and experiences that are occurring. It cuts us off from life, shuts us down, and robs us of experiencing anything. Shame is one of the most formidable culprits for tipping us outside of our window of tolerance, and tipping outside of our window is extremely fertile ground for using.

From the diagram, you may notice that whether your tendency is to hyperactivate or to deactivate, both provide perfect ingredients for the recipe of addiction. When we lose our emotional balance and equilibrium, the way in which we interact with other people tends to create disconnection. Given that these moments occur when we are emotionally flooded, we lose the option of reaching out for support and leaning into the people closest to us when we need them the most. That is extremely problematic when it comes to shame. Shame requires bringing the darkness of pain into the light of the people who care about us.

Do You Hyperactivate or Deactivate?

Circle the following items that you *most* identify with when you experience shame or intense emotion.

Hyperactivate	**Deactivate**
Restlessness	Social isolation
Fidgeting	Avoiding situations
Hypervigilance	Emotional numbing
Active startle response	Dissociating
Emotional reactivity, lashing out	Passive behavior
Impulsivity	People pleasing
Agitation	Rarely speaking up
Racing thoughts	Avoiding making decisions
Frequently interrupting people	Shutting down
Overwhelmed by stimuli such as light, sound, movement	A lack of initiating

Which column did you find most of your answers in? Identifying these experiences in the moment that they occur will increase your ability to find your way back to a state of balance and equilibrium.

Pay attention as often as possible to your emotional state throughout the day. Become more acquainted with your inner terrain. The more aware you become of your emotional experience, the less frequently your emotions will ambush you, and knock you out of your window of tolerance. There is a huge difference between you having your emotions, and your emotions having you. This is a powerful tool for keeping you on the path to transform your relationship with addiction.

Inner Resourcing

As you embark on the next part of your journey to uncover the shame that is buried deep inside of you, it will be important to have emotional rebalancing tools at your disposal. These are the practices you have hopefully using to move back into balance with yourself whenever you feel off-center:

- Taking your emotional temperature (chapter 3)

- Three-part breath (chapter 3)

- Quiet contemplation

- Journaling (introduction)

Additionally, we have explored useful concepts and experiences throughout the book that serve as additional tools:

- Proactively identifying your triggers (chapter 5)

- Understanding and identifying emotions (chapter 7)

- Tracking negative narratives (chapter 6)

All these skill builders are designed to increase your awareness of the kinds of experiences that may throw you off balance. Practice them. Prior to doing the next series of exercises, select two techniques that you most reliably utilize to regain your emotional balance. Feel free to deliberately practice them all so that you can pick the two that are most effective for you. Experiment with these over the next few days before continuing with this chapter.

Now that you have been experimenting with resourcing yourself and increasing your awareness of your emotional world, let's take the next logical step on the path: using attachment and EFT to work through the shame that drives your addiction.

Uncovering Shame

Return to the "Identify Your Spheres of Influence" exercise in chapter 3. Identify the world that has been the most impactful in creating the deeply held negative beliefs you hold about your identity:

- Relational world, which includes your relationships

- Cultural world, which includes your identity and community

- World at large, which includes current and world events

First get centered: Take five three-part breaths to stabilize your nervous system.

Next, review what you wrote in that exercise regarding the impact that sphere of influence has had on your sense of worth, safety, and hope. Expand upon your answers by responding to the following prompts, being aware of the shame narrative that is always running in the background for you.

This is what I hear when the voice of shame starts talking: _____

_____

_____

_____

_____

Notice what is happening inside as you identify your shame narrative and write it out:

_____

_____

_____

_____

_____

_____

_____

Taking the Power out of Shame

As you already know, shame gains its power by hiding in silence. Much like dissolving deep dark secrets by finally sharing them with somebody out loud, we disempower shame by taking the risk to share the parts of ourselves that we find unlovable with someone who genuinely cares about us.

Attachment is the ultimate remedy for breaking free from the cycle of shame. When we have been wounded in relationship; we need to heal through relationship. We must allow ourselves to face the fear, lean into shame, and invite caring people to hold it with us. Then we can finally release the toxic emotions that bind us. By bringing shame to the light of love, we not only disempower shame, but we also disempower addiction. When we release shame into the light of care and compassion with the people we love, we are free. _Connection becomes the substitute replacement for addiction._ Addiction is no longer required to contain the monster in the box. Through the courage to face our fears—and the responsiveness of other people's care and compassion—we can transform our relationship to addiction once and for all.

Shame Busting

Now the time has come to finally take the fangs out of the shame that has been viciously gnawing away at you for most of your lifetime. The personal growth work that you have been courageously doing has taken you to the point of accessing, identifying, and beginning to process the parts of yourself that even you have struggled with loving and accepting.

1. **Planning:** Decide upon a quiet space for this conversation. Find a time when your schedule is unencumbered with other demands on your time and attention. Select an important person in your life with whom to share your narrative. Let this person know that you would like to have a very meaningful conversation with them. Tell them that you are simply asking them to be themselves and hold space for you. You are not asking for advice, solutions, or for them to fix anything.

If you cannot identify a person in your life for this exercise, then reconnect with your imagined ideal attachment figure from earlier in the book. Find a quiet place to relax, turn your awareness inward, and reenvision all the wonderful qualities in your attachment figure. Feel their presence with you. Partake in the following aspects of this exercise as it is written and allow yourself to experience the relational receptivity of each step. Write out your plan below.

_____

_____

_____

_____

_____

2. **On-ramping:** Thank this significant person for their willingness to be part of your healing process. Let them know how much it means to you. Feel their presence and take in all the wonderful qualities they possess that went into you selecting them to begin with. Prior to sharing, begin by letting them know how hard this is to do. Confide in them about your concerns and share your fears. Write down a few ideas of how you could broach this topic.

_____

_____

_____

_____

_____

3. **Executing:** Take a leap of faith to share what you've been carrying in these hidden compartments inside of yourself for all these years. If you are comfortable, let them know what the source of your shame narrative is and how it has kept you in hiding. Do your best to make eye contact so that you can soak in their interest, presence, patience, and care. Take this in. Share your narrative.

_____

_____

_____

_____

4. **Processing:** Having taken such an enormous risk by sharing parts of you that you most likely have never confided in anyone about before, ask if the other person is willing to share what it means to them for you to have confided in them so deeply. Feel free to ask them what they are aware of inside of them as you lean into them so openly. Enjoy a nice conversation about leaning in and reaching for connection around something that you have had to carry alone for a lifetime. Soak in the goodness of this moment. When the conversation concludes, be ready thank your partner. When you have a few moments after this conversation has taken place, write down what it was like for you to risk so courageously.

    _____

    _____

    _____

    _____

    _____

5. **Observe:** Write down what you notice over the next few days as you reflect on the impact of taking this risk, and how you may explore risking and sharing in the future.

    _____

    _____

    _____

    _____

    _____

You have now taken the cumulative process of the work you have been doing throughout this book and applied it to the greatest risk of all: releasing your shame. Be aware that this is not a "one and done" experience. It is something to be continued. It deepens your strength and wisdom over time. Rome wasn't built in a day.

I have immense admiration for your willingness to travel this path. This is the key to transforming your relationship with addiction. Whether your choice is toward abstinence or some form of moderation management, remember the journey itself is the true destination. The door to your inner journey is now wide open. You are on the path, and there is no turning back. Although the work can be difficult at times, the results are extraordinarily beneficial and life-giving. This work is transformative. It changed my life forever, now you are equipped to change yours. I would like to offer you my personal congratulations for the strength of character and integrity required to do this work. Way to go!

CHAPTER 13

Consolidation: Where to Go from Here

You have covered a lot of ground since you first opened the pages of this book. Huge congratulations to you for your commitment and perseverance to genuinely transform your relationship to addiction. You may have noticed that this book is unique in that it has guided you on a journey to approach your addictive process from the inside out.

Addiction is not random. It doesn't occur in a vacuum. If we are consistently alone when the shit hits the fan, taking the edge off the isolation and pain with addiction isn't such a crazy idea.

When people are well resourced with circles of caring others in their world, the likelihood of getting caught in addiction when life goes sideways is relatively low (Flores 2011). Reaching out and leaning into people who genuinely care about us during moments of distress allows us to metabolize our hurt and pain. This is how we process life's challenges. The connection that we have with others in these moments allows us to thoroughly process difficult events. It supports us in letting go of painful emotional residue that would otherwise build up inside of us and diminish our lives. Additionally, securely attached relationships support us in acquiring wisdom and know-how to successfully navigate the trials and tribulations of life without the need for substances or addictive behaviors.

These experiences provide a profound secondary benefit: they transmit the powerful meta message that *we matter*. We internalize the trust that people will be there for us when we need them, and therefore we conclude that we must have intrinsic value. This is secure attachment. When feel good about ourselves from the inside out and trust our abilities to confidently face the ups and downs of life, then there is no need or place for addiction. Having transformed our relationship with addiction from the inside out allows us to live in the presence of joy, happiness, and a lovely sense of well-being.

You have taken the leap of faith to embark upon the journey of self-discovery to finally get your arms around what has been driving your addiction so that you can transform your relationship with addiction once and for all. The exercises for self-reflection, emotional awareness, and engaging with EFT processes have all been geared to intimately acquaint you with yourself. Your clear understanding about what makes you tick sheds light upon the reasons for why you needed addictive processes in the first place. Clarity about your addictive process offers you options for coping more compassionately with your inner world so that you will not need to rely upon your substances of choice to do so for you. In essence, this entire journey has been about transforming your relationship with yourself.

Takeaways from Your Journey

Even now, having come so far in our medical understanding of addiction, the negative and judgmental stigmas regarding people caught in the tailspin of addiction still exist (Stauffer 2020). Sometimes the stigma can be internalized, and we become mired in self-judgment. I hope that working with addictive processes from the inside out has allowed you to see yourself with much more empathy and compassion.

The inside-out journey through addiction is intended to generate compassion and empathy toward yourself through illuminating the human face that remains hidden behind addiction. Addiction simply attempted to provide a very understandable function for you: it stood in as a substitute replacement for the love and care that was not an option during times of challenge.

Which experiences of the ideas, themes and exercises from this book helped you to see yourself with more compassion, care, and understanding?

_____

_____

_____

_____

_____

_____

_____

_____

_____

Your efforts in this book have exhibited the purest form of bravery. It is not for the faint of heart. However, much like the revered swordsmiths of old, the finest and strongest blades were expertly forged by being placed in the fire over and over again. This is precisely what you have done. You have leaned into the heat. You have leaned into parts of yourself you may not have even known existed (for good reason). You have allowed yourself to open the door and walk through the flames of the unprocessed emotional worlds that have resided within you for many years. You are undoubtedly better for having done so. This is the process of personal growth.

Acquainting Yourself with Your Inner Emotional World

Along the way, you have learned a lot about yourself. You are more keenly aware of what makes you tick and what you have been self-medicating with addiction. You have also developed a new sense of clarity about your inner world that did not exist before. Through differentiating the components of your emotional experience through the lens of EFT, you clarified the specific situations and events that formed the starting point of your addictive process. In other words, addiction didn't just "happen."

And lastly, you were able to clearly understand the purpose of your addictive behavior: a perpetual attempt to keep a lid on that compartment. Each of the components of emotion—the cues, inner narratives, feelings, and action tendencies—has provided you multiple doorways to access your inner world. Your newfound awareness of what you are going through when a cue triggers you will assist in understanding what you need in those difficult moments to regulate distress. This is the royal road for moving beyond self-medicating with addiction.

How would you summarize your addictive process through the four components of emotion (cues, inner narratives, feelings, and action tendencies)?

_____

_____

_____

_____

_____

Learning the language of emotion through the lens of attachment may have also put you squarely in touch with the meanings that you internalized about life. It is one thing to know that you may not have had the reliable support, love, and care you deserved. It is quite another thing to have challenged yourself to reflect upon the impact it had.

Write a few sentences that really get to the heart of your takeaways of how a lack of secure attachment in your life affected your sense of self, others, and the world.

This is how the lack of secure attachment in my life affected the way I feel about:

Myself: _____

_____

_____

_____

_____

Others: _____

_____

_____

_____

_____

The world: _____

_____

_____

_____

_____

Additionally, you found the humility to explore how you may have contributed to creating obstacles to having securely attached relationships in your life. Doing so required genuine strength of character.

Through more clearly understanding the ways in which you expressed yourself in stressful moments, you were able to consider more meaningful ways of directly expressing yourself to others. This increases the chance that you will feel understood, and the people close to you will have a better chance of responding directly to your needs for love, support, and understanding.

Write a sentence or two about how you were getting in your own way:

_____

_____

_____

Write what you discovered when you applied new, more-effective ways of communicating with the important people in your life, when things are stressful:

_____

_____

_____

_____

You are defining how to use new, healthy attachment strategies to reach out, lean in, and connect with others in moments when you need support. You are effectively putting attachment into action! Well done!

Transforming Your Relationship to Addiction

The skills, groups, and treatment options that are most available to those of us struggling with addiction have been based on either untested premises or from research done in clinical settings particularly with people who have already been in treatment. In other words, they look at a very small sample of the people who really struggle with addiction like you and me (Kean 2013; Finberg 2015).

What has been sadly ignored or placed outside of the field of therapy and personal growth is results of research from epidemiological studies (National Institutes of Health 2006; Blanco et al. 2011). These massive studies have been conducted by randomly selecting a cross-section of people around the country, most of whom have never had any formal addiction treatment. The results they yielded are stunning! As a matter of fact, the results offer us incredibly great news: in time most people struggling with addiction stop on their own without formal intervention.

These two camps have created infighting as to what the best recommendations are for how people should approach recovery. The first category feels strongly that recovery, full recovery, requires abstinence.

The second category approaches recovery through *moderation management*. Moderation management examines the impact of moderate, or social using, on people's quality of life. In other words, the second body of research noted that despite having met the clinical criteria for substance use dependence at some point in their life, their using habits over the previous year or more no longer met the criteria and their lives were going smoothly without detrimental effects from moderate usage.

This book does not prescribe or recommend either approach for everybody. It is crucial that you select a path that works for you. This requires you to be able to honestly evaluate the impact of using on your life. Does using affect your health? Does using affect your relationships? Has using caused legal problems and consequences? Does using send your marriage or relationship into a tailspin? Has using affected your work performance? Does it affect your mood detrimentally? These are all incredibly important questions.

Abstinence is recommended when you answer yes to the questions above. It is also essential if your using has become life-threatening or threatens the well-being of others. In our primary relationships, using may have created attachment injuries, horrific breaches of trust, or significant interpersonal harm. If this is the case, your relationship will not be able to tolerate using, and you will be faced with the question of whether you want your drug of choice or your relationship. The choice is yours. Please use the following chart to examine the consequences of your using so that you can determine which path of recovery will work best for you. You can also visit http://www.newharbinger.com/52403 to print copies of this chart to complete at different times along your journey.

How Does My Addictive Process Negatively Affect Me?

	NO	YES	IF YES, HOW?
My physical health?			
My mental or emotional health?			
My friendships or family relationships?			
My marriage or partnership?			
My legal status?			
My vocational status or performance?			
Can I maintain the limits I set to contain my using?			

If you responded "yes" to several questions, you may want to consider abstinence. These categories comprise major aspects of our lives. If addiction is negatively impacting even one of them in a very significant way, and you have doubts about being able to have a different outcome, then abstinence may be the best path for you.

If you checked fewer than two boxes and the impact of using on your life has been minimal, while the other important areas of your life are going quite well, then perhaps moderation management could be your path. Again, the most important qualifier is which path works best for you. Recovery is not a one-size-fits-all process.

Life and Recovery Is a Journey Rather Than a Destination

You have embraced your commitment to more than just simply recovery. You have embraced your commitment to life. Your life. This book has been an invitation to follow the path of the hero's journey inward. It is the most difficult and hands down the most beneficial and remarkable work that any human being could ever take on. It is transformative. Through this work you will gain personal strength and wisdom that will remain with you throughout the course of your entire life.

I hope you have come to accept that none of us can do it alone. If you were able to find significant others with whom you can confide the fruits of your labors, I hope it has been an uplifting and an encouraging experience.

However, some of us have endured more than most. These rivers run extraordinarily deep. To continue your journey, a strong recommendation would be to find a very good attachment oriented, or EFT therapist well versed in addiction, and who practices what is known as trauma-informed therapy. A person possessing these qualifications would be an incredible guide to walk alongside you while you let go of the heaviness of the difficult times in your life. Trauma and shame are very sticky. People well trained in attachment psychotherapy or EFT can help you access, face, process, and work through the emotional intensity that may still be lingering after you turn the final page of this book.

As mentioned before, this entire book has been about transforming your relationship with yourself. That's the ultimate transformation. That is the journey that we will all be on until we breathe our final exhalation in life. Embrace it! Lean into it! Give yourself the gift of *recovery*. You will be delighted to have done so.

Author's Note

The processes, concepts, practices, and exercises throughout this book have been the heart and soul of my own journey. They helped me take an honest look at myself and provided me with the strength, wisdom, and ability to encounter and finally face the hidden compartments within me. I didn't do it alone. I found a lot of support. I logged a lot of miles in my own therapy, and in time I was able to identify people who were wiser and stronger, who had walked the path before me. They believed in me. They helped me to believe in myself.

The world I inhabit currently is unrecognizable to what my life looked like when I was caught in the clutches of addiction. Therefore, I offer you the same path that has been so profoundly transformative to me and thousands of other people.

Thank you very much for allowing me to be your guide and walk alongside you as you begin the hero's journey. I know that your dreams can come true, and you can be exactly the kind of person you genuinely want to be. You are a superstar. We all are. We must give ourselves the chance to shine. So...let yourself shine!

References

Alexander, B. K. 2008. *The Globalization of Addiction: A Study in Poverty of the Spirit.* Oxford: Oxford University Press.

Blanco, C., C. Lopez-Quintero, D. S. Hasin, J. P. de Los Cobos, A. Pines, S. Wang, and B. F. Grant. 2011. "Probability and Predictors of Remission from Lifetime Nicotine, Alcohol, Cannabis, or Cocaine Dependence: Results from the National Epidemiologic Survey on Alcohol and Related Conditions." *Society for the Study of Addiction* 106(3): 657–669.

Cassidy, J., D. J. Jones, and P. R. Shaver. 2013. "Contributions of Attachment Theory and Research: A Framework for Future Research, Translation, and Policy." *Development and Psychopathology* 25(4): 1415–1434.

Erozkan, A. 2016. "The Link Between Types of Attachment and Childhood Trauma." *Universal Journal of Educational Research* 4.

Felitti, V. J. 2002. "The Relation Between Adverse Childhood Experiences and Adult Health: Turning Gold into Lead." *Permanente Journal* 6(1): 44–47.

Flores, P. J. 2011. *Addiction as an Attachment Disorder.* Lanham, MD: Jason Aronson.

Greenspan, M. 2004. *Healing Through the Dark Emotions: The Wisdom of Grief, Fear, and Despair.* Boulder: Shambala Publications.

Griffin, D. W., and K. Bartholomew. 1994. "The Metaphysics of Measurement: The Case of Adult Attachment." In *Attachment Processes in Adulthood*, edited by K. Bartholomew and D. Perlman, 17–52. London: Jessica Kingsley Publishers.

Hasin, D. S., F. S. Stinson, E. Ogburn, and B. F. Grant. 2007. "Prevalence, Correlates, Disability, and Comorbidity of DSM Alcohol Abuse in the United States: Result from the National Epidemiological Survey on Alcohol and Related Conditions." *Archives of General Psychiatry* 64(7): 830–842.

Heyman, G. 2009. *Addiction: A Disorder of Choice.* Boston: Harvard University Press.

Johnson, S. M. 2005. *Emotionally Focused Couple Therapy with Trauma Survivors: Strengthening Attachment Bonds.* New York: Guilford Press.

———. 2019. *Attachment Theory in Practice: Emotionally Focused Therapy (EFT) with Individuals, Couples, and Families.* New York: Guilford Press.

Finberg, A., dir. 2015. *The Business of Recovery.* Los Angeles: Greg Horvath Productions; Distribber.

Kean, J. 2013. "Why the US Fails at Treating Addiction." Life Science, November 27. https://www.livescience.com/41557-why-america-fails-at-addiction-treatment.html.

Lange, W. R., L. DePadilla, E. Parker, and K. Holland. 2024. "Substance Use, and Substance Use Disorders." *CDC Yellow Book.* https://wwwnc.cdc.gov/travel/yellowbook/2024/additional-considerations/substance-use.

Maté, G. 2007. *In the Realm of Hungry Ghosts: Close Encounters with Addiction.* Berkeley: North Atlantic Books.

McLaughlin, K. A., P. Berglund, M. J. Gruber, R. C. Kessler, N. A. Sampson, and A. M. Zaslavsky. 2011. "Recovery from PTSD Following Hurricane Katrina." *Journal of Depression and Anxiety* 28(6): 439–446.

National Center for Health Statistics. 2021. "Health, United States, 2020–2021: Drug Overdose Deaths." CDC. https://www.cdc.gov/nchs/hus/topics/drug-overdose-deaths.htm.

National Institutes of Health. "Alcohol Use and Alcohol Use Disorders in the United States: Main Findings from the 2001–2002 National Epidemiologic Survey on Alcohol and Related Conditions (NESARC)." *U.S. Alcohol Epidemiologic Data Reference Manual* 8(1).

Neria, Y., L. DiGrande, and B. G. Adams. 2011. "Post Traumatic Stress Disorder Following the September 11, 2001 Terrorist Attacks. A Review of the Literature Among Highly Exposed Populations." *American Psychologist* 66(6): 429–446.

Rabin, R. C. 2021. "Overdose Deaths Reached Record High as the Pandemic Spread." *New York Times,* November 17. https://www.nytimes.com/2021/11/17/health/drug-overdoses-fentanyl-deaths.html.

Salter Ainsworth, M. D., M. C. Blehar, E. Waters, and S. N. Wall. 2015. *Patterns of Attachment: A Psychological Study of the Strange Situation.* London: Psychology Press.

Spengler, P. M., N. A. Lee, S. A. Wiebe, and A. K. Wittenborn. 2022. "A Comprehensive Meta-Analysis on the Efficacy of Emotionally Focused Couple Therapy." *Couple and Family Psychology: Research and Practice.* https://doi.org/10.1037/cfp0000233.

Stauffer, W. 2020. "Addiction Treatment Is Broken. Here's What It Should Look Like." *STAT,* January 2. https://www.statnews.com/2020/01/02/addiction-treatment-is-broken-heres-what-it-should-look-like.

Swedo, E. A., M. V. Aslam, L. L. Dahlberg, P. Holditch Niolon, A. S. Guinn, T. R. Simon, and J. A. Mercy. 2023. "Prevalence of Adverse Childhood Experiences Among US Adults—Behavioral Risk Factor Surveillance System, 2011–2020." *Morbidity and Mortality Weekly Report* 72(26): 707–715.

van der Kolk, B. 2015. *The Body Keeps the Score: Brain, Mind, and Body in the Healing of Trauma.* New York: Penguin Books.

Watson, H. 2023. *Conquering PTSD.* Osawatomie, KS: Jelly Bean Press.

Weissman, N., S. V. Batten, K. D. Rheem, S. A. Wiebe, R. M. Pasillas, W. Potts, M. Barone, C. H. Brown, and L. B. Dixon. 2018. "The Effectiveness of Emotionally Focused Couples Therapy with Veterans with PTSD: A Pilot Study." *Journal of Couple and Relationship Therapy* 17(1): 25–41.

Wittenborn, A. K., T. Liu, T. A. Ridenour, E. M. Lachmar, E. Rouleau, and R. B. Seedall. 2018. "Randomized Controlled Trial of Emotionally Focused Couple Therapy Compared to Treatment as Usual for Depression: Outcomes and Mechanisms of Change." *Journal of Marital and Family Therapy* 45: 395–409.

Michael Barnett, LPCC, is a certified trainer in emotionally focused therapy (EFT) who has added to the canon of EFT training by helping clinicians work more effectively with trauma and addiction through the EFT lens. Barnett specializes in the use of EFT as a humanistic/experiential, attachment-based therapy to transform clients' relationship with their addictive processes. He is codirector of the Emotionally Focused Therapy Center of Los Angeles, and founder of the Atlanta Community for Emotionally Focused Therapy. He resides in La Crescenta, CA.

Foreword writer **Susan Johnson, EdD** (1947–2024), was a therapist, author, and the pioneering innovator of emotionally focused therapy (EFT). Johnson received many awards over her lifetime, including the Order of Canada. She was named "Psychologist of the Year" in 2016 by Division 43 of the American Psychological Association, and was recognized by the American Association for Marriage and Family Therapy for Outstanding Contribution to the Field of Couple and Family Therapy. Her work has left an indelible mark on the field of therapy and the lives of countless individuals, couples, and families worldwide.

Real change *is* possible

For more than forty-five years, New Harbinger has published proven-effective self-help books and pioneering workbooks to help readers of all ages and backgrounds improve mental health and well-being, and achieve lasting personal growth. In addition, our spirituality books offer profound guidance for deepening awareness and cultivating healing, self-discovery, and fulfillment.

Founded by psychologist Matthew McKay and Patrick Fanning, New Harbinger is proud to be an independent, employee-owned company. Our books reflect our core values of integrity, innovation, commitment, sustainability, compassion, and trust. Written by leaders in the field and recommended by therapists worldwide, New Harbinger books are practical, accessible, and provide real tools for real change.

 **newharbinger**publications

MORE BOOKS from
NEW HARBINGER PUBLICATIONS

**THE EMDR WORKBOOK
FOR TRAUMA AND PTSD**

Skills to Manage Triggers, Move
Beyond Traumatic Memories,
and Take Back Your Life

978-1684039586 / US $24.95

**ADULT SURVIVORS OF
TOXIC FAMILY MEMBERS**

Tools to Maintain Boundaries,
Deal with Criticism, and Heal from
Shame After Ties Have Been Cut

978-1684039289 / US $17.95

**DISTRESS TOLERANCE
MADE EASY**

Dialectical Behavior Therapy Skills
for Dealing with Intense Emotions
in Difficult Times

978-1648482373 / US $18.95

**THE MINDFULNESS
AND ACCEPTANCE
WORKBOOK FOR ANXIETY,
SECOND EDITION**

A Guide to Breaking Free from
Anxiety, Phobias, and Worry Using
Acceptance and Commitment Therapy

978-1626253346 / US $24.95

**THE SELF-COMPASSION
DAILY JOURNAL**

Let Go of Your Inner Critic and
Embrace Who You Are with
Acceptance and Commitment Therapy

978-1648482496 / US $18.95

**SETTING BOUNDARIES
THAT STICK**

How Neurobiology Can Help You
Rewire Your Brain to Feel Safe,
Connected, and Empowered

978-1648481291 / US $18.95

new harbinger publications

1-800-748-6273 / newharbinger.com

(VISA, MC, AMEX / prices subject to change without notice)

Follow Us 📷 📘 🐦 ▶ 📌 💼 ♪ ⓖ

Don't miss out on new books from New Harbinger.
Subscribe to our email list at **newharbinger.com/subscribe**

Did you know there are **free tools** you can download for this book?

Free tools are things like **worksheets, guided meditation exercises**, and **more** that will help you get the most out of your book.

You can download free tools for this book— whether you bought or borrowed it, in any format, from any source—from the New Harbinger website. All you need is a NewHarbinger.com account. Just use the URL provided in this book to view the free tools that are available for it. Then, click on the "download" button for the free tool you want, and follow the prompts that appear to log in to your NewHarbinger.com account and download the material.

You can also save the free tools for this book to your **Free Tools Library** so you can access them again anytime, just by logging in to your account! Just look for this button on the book's free tools page.

+ Save this to my free tools library